QlikView Essentials

Want to solve your Business Intelligence headaches?
Learn how QlikView can help, and discover a powerful
yet accessible BI solution that lets you harness your data

Chandraish Sinha

BIRMINGHAM - MUMBAI

QlikView Essentials

First published: January 2016

Production reference: 1120116

Published by Packt Publishing Ltd.
Livery Place
35 Livery Street
Birmingham B3 2PB, UK.

ISBN 978-1-78439-728-9

www.packtpub.com

Credits

Author
Chandraish Sinha

Reviewer
Julián Villafuerte

Commissioning Editor
Akram Hussain

Acquisition Editors
Purav Motiwalla

Larissa Pinto

Content Development Editor
Samantha Gonsalves

Technical Editor
Pramod Kumavat

Copy Editor
Joanna McMahon

Project Coordinator
Kinjal Bari

Proofreader
Safis Editing

Indexer
Rekha Nair

Graphics
Kirk D'Penha

Production Coordinator
Manu Joseph

Cover Work
Manu Joseph

About the Author

Chandraish Sinha is a Business Intelligence enthusiast from Ohio. He brings 17 years of experience in providing cost-effective BI solutions.

He is responsible for many QlikView implementations in various industries, namely financial, insurance, pharmaceuticals, and event management. He currently holds QlikView Designer and QlikView Developer certifications.

He shares his knowledge and passion through his QlikView blog (http://www.learnallbi.com/).

He currently works as an independent BI consultant and helps organizations in implementing BI solutions.

I would like to thank my family and friends to provide me time and encouragement in the process of writing this book.

About the Reviewer

Julián Villafuerte is a founding member of Evolution Consulting, a Mexican firm, which provides QlikView consulting services throughout America. Since 2010, he has helped several companies to define effective strategies for data management and business analysis. As a consultant, he has worked in application development, project management, presales, and training divisions for many industries, including retail, manufacturing, and insurance.

In October, 2015, he published *Creating Stunning Dashboards with QlikView, Packt Publishing*, a practical handbook focused on developing useful and engaging analytical applications. He has a Master's degree in Information Technology Management and teaches at the Tecnológico de Monterrey in Mexico City. Recently, he started a blog named QlikFreak (https://qlikfreak.wordpress.com/), where he shares tips and tricks about data visualization, scripting, and best practices.

www.PacktPub.com

Support files, eBooks, discount offers, and more

For support files and downloads related to your book, please visit www.PacktPub.com.

Did you know that Packt offers eBook versions of every book published, with PDF and ePub files available? You can upgrade to the eBook version at www.PacktPub.com and as a print book customer, you are entitled to a discount on the eBook copy. Get in touch with us at service@packtpub.com for more details.

At www.PacktPub.com, you can also read a collection of free technical articles, sign up for a range of free newsletters and receive exclusive discounts and offers on Packt books and eBooks.

https://www2.packtpub.com/books/subscription/packtlib

Do you need instant solutions to your IT questions? PacktLib is Packt's online digital book library. Here, you can search, access, and read Packt's entire library of books.

Why subscribe?

- Fully searchable across every book published by Packt
- Copy and paste, print, and bookmark content
- On demand and accessible via a web browser

Free access for Packt account holders

If you have an account with Packt at www.PacktPub.com, you can use this to access PacktLib today and view 9 entirely free books. Simply use your login credentials for immediate access.

Instant updates on new Packt books

Get notified! Find out when new books are published by following @PacktEnterprise on Twitter or the *Packt Enterprise* Facebook page.

Table of Contents

Preface

The data is growing at a higher pace so does the need to understand data. There are many applications that perform data analysis and design, but QlikView takes Business Intelligence to the next level. The ability of QlikView to extract and present the data in a way that the human mind thinks, has made QlikView hugely popular. The associative nature of the QlikView data model has made business discovery fairly simple.

This book is being designed in a way that provides equal value to a novice BI developer and a seasoned practitioner. This book starts with the basics of QlikView, data warehousing and works through creating data models and visualizations. This book covers all the topics for the QlikView designer and developer and can be used as a reference guide in new or ongoing implementations.

Each chapter in the book follows a structure:

- Each chapter will cover the essentials of the topic in the chapter.
- This book covers both QlikView developer/Data model and QlikView designer/visualization topics.
- Each topic is explained first and then followed by a step–by-step exercise. Readers can follow these exercises to create their own data model and dash boarding application.
- This book uses the Adventure Works database; most readers will have familiarity with this database. There is tons of information available online on this database, so users will easily understand.
- This book also comes with data in MS Access, Excel, and text files. It is also accompanied with QlikView solutions/qvw's that the reader can download and follow.

What this book covers

Chapter 1, QlikView Essentials, provides the basics of QlikView. It gives an overview of the QlikView architecture. It also provides instructions on how to download QlikView. You get to know about the star schema and learn about the underlining data model used in the book.

Chapter 2, Extract, Transform, and Load, as the name suggests, dives into building a data model in QlikView by extracting, transforming, and loading data. In this chapter, readers will learn about using scripts to load data from different sources and data transformation.

Chapter 3, Optimizing Your Data Model, deals with techniques to optimize a data model. This involves different ways to join data and data aggregation.

Chapter 4, Data Modeling Challenges, helps you in understanding and resolving different data modeling challenges. You learn about loading some special table types. You will also learn about the best practices of data modeling.

Chapter 5, Creating Dashboards, gives you the opportunity to learn about different dash boarding practices and create different visualization objects.

Chapter 6, Comparative Analysis, enforces the importance of data comparison in the dashboards using Set Analysis and Alternate State. You also learn about implementing what-if analysis.

Chapter 7, Securing Your Application, teaches how to secure your dashboard application.

Chapter 8, Application Deployment, provides an overview of servers and how applications can be deployed on the server.

What you need for this book

To follow this book, QlikView Desktop is required. QlikView desktop can be downloaded for free from Qlik.com by following the steps in *Chapter 1, QlikView Essentials.* To run QlikView desktop, you will need a minimum of 2 GB RAM and 2 GB of hard disk. Windows 7 or higher is recommended. Though not compulsory, knowledge of Business Intelligence terms and SQL knowledge will be helpful.

Who this book is for

This book covers all the essentials of QlikView application building. The book is written for novice developers who want to learn building dashboard applications using QlikView. This book will also help developers who are working on other applications but want to adopt QlikView as a next step in their career. This book covers all the aspects of QlikView from developers and designers to deployment.

Conventions

In this book, you will find a number of text styles that distinguish between different kinds of information. Here are some examples of these styles and an explanation of their meaning.

Code words in text, database table names, folder names, filenames, file extensions, pathnames, dummy URLs, user input, and Twitter handles are shown as follows: "After loading this statement drop `%TempKeyField` as it was required only for comparison."

A block of code is set as follows:

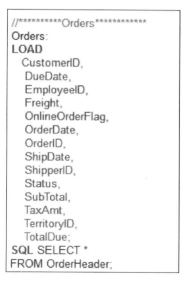

```
//***********Orders***********
Orders:
LOAD
    CustomerID,
    DueDate,
    EmployeeID,
    Freight,
    OnlineOrderFlag,
    OrderDate,
    OrderID,
    ShipDate,
    ShipperID,
    Status,
    SubTotal,
    TaxAmt,
    TerritoryID,
    TotalDue;
SQL SELECT *
FROM OrderHeader;
```

New terms and **important words** are shown in bold. Words that you see on the screen, for example, in menus or dialog boxes, appear in the text like this: "Use **Debug** option from **File** menu to debug your script."

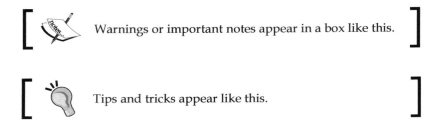

Warnings or important notes appear in a box like this.

Tips and tricks appear like this.

Reader feedback

Feedback from our readers is always welcome. Let us know what you think about this book—what you liked or disliked. Reader feedback is important for us as it helps us develop titles that you will really get the most out of.

To send us general feedback, simply e-mail feedback@packtpub.com, and mention the book's title in the subject of your message.

If there is a topic that you have expertise in and you are interested in either writing or contributing to a book, see our author guide at www.packtpub.com/authors.

Customer support

Now that you are the proud owner of a Packt book, we have a number of things to help you to get the most from your purchase.

Downloading the example code

You can download the example code files from your account at http://www.packtpub.com for all the Packt Publishing books you have purchased. If you purchased this book elsewhere, you can visit http://www.packtpub.com/support and register to have the files e-mailed directly to you.

Errata

Although we have taken every care to ensure the accuracy of our content, mistakes do happen. If you find a mistake in one of our books—maybe a mistake in the text or the code—we would be grateful if you could report this to us. By doing so, you can save other readers from frustration and help us improve subsequent versions of this book. If you find any errata, please report them by visiting http://www.packtpub. com/submit-errata, selecting your book, clicking on the **Errata Submission Form** link, and entering the details of your errata. Once your errata are verified, your submission will be accepted and the errata will be uploaded to our website or added to any list of existing errata under the Errata section of that title.

To view the previously submitted errata, go to https://www.packtpub.com/books/content/support and enter the name of the book in the search field. The required information will appear under the **Errata** section.

Piracy

Piracy of copyrighted material on the Internet is an ongoing problem across all media. At Packt, we take the protection of our copyright and licenses very seriously. If you come across any illegal copies of our works in any form on the Internet, please provide us with the location address or website name immediately so that we can pursue a remedy.

Please contact us at copyright@packtpub.com with a link to the suspected pirated material.

We appreciate your help in protecting our authors and our ability to bring you valuable content.

Questions

If you have a problem with any aspect of this book, you can contact us at questions@packtpub.com, and we will do our best to address the problem.

1
QlikView Fundamentals

If you are reading this book, then you are already familiar with the power of QlikView. You are on your way to utilize the in-memory and associative power of QlikView to build better insights for your organization. Business intelligence applications developed in QlikView are helping organizations worldwide in transforming their raw data into useful information.

Before jumping into creating data transformations and visualization in QlikView, we will cover the basics of this book. This book will cover all the essentials of QlikView designer and developer concepts. It will start with basics of QlikView, and then dive into loading data, performing transformations, creating visualizations, and deployment of the application. In each chapter, you will understand the key concepts and follow step-by-step exercises.

The first chapter will cover the development life cycle of QlikView, an introduction to a fictitious company Adventure works Inc., and an introduction to the adventure works data model.

In this chapter, we will learn about:

- QlikView components and installation
- QlikView basics
- Problem definition of a fictitious company
- Understanding existing data model and tables
- Development environment setup

QlikView components

QlikView has three main components: QlikView Desktop, QlikView Server (QVS), and QlikView Publisher.

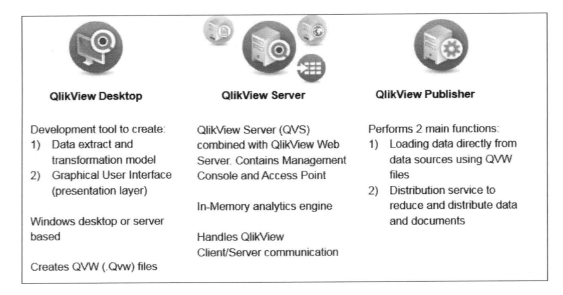

QlikView Desktop

Development tool to create:
1) Data extract and transformation model
2) Graphical User Interface (presentation layer)

Windows desktop or server based

Creates QVW (.Qvw) files

QlikView Server

QlikView Server (QVS) combined with QlikView Web Server. Contains Management Console and Access Point

In-Memory analytics engine

Handles QlikView Client/Server communication

QlikView Publisher

Performs 2 main functions:
1) Loading data directly from data sources using QVW files
2) Distribution service to reduce and distribute data and documents

In this book, we will use QlikView desktop to create data model and visualizations.

QlikView installation

To explore the power of QlikView, you need to install QlikView desktop. A personal edition of QlikView desktop can be downloaded from http://www.qlik.com/us/explore/products/free-download?ga-link=navbtn.

You will be asked to register, or login if you are already a registered user.

The installation file comes in 32-bit and 64-bit editions. Install the version based on your computer's specification. Installation is very straightforward. You need to just follow the default options. The personal edition has the full capability of QlikView desktop. The Personal edition works with local files only; you cannot share your application design file (qvw) with another unregistered user, or load a design file from another user.

Installation comes with an `Examples` folder that contains QlikView documents. You can review this folder to learn more about QlikView. This folder is located in your installation path under `C:\Program Files\QlikView`.

Before moving further, we will learn the basics of QlikView:

- Technology: QlikView uses an in-memory data model. It stores all the data in RAM instead of disk. RAM storage results in faster response time.

- Associative experience: In QlikView, data is always associated. Association is automatically created between two tables having common field names. The associative technology results in an enhanced data discovery experience. Traditional BI solutions follow a predefined path to navigate and explore the data. QlikView allows users to take any data path of their choice.

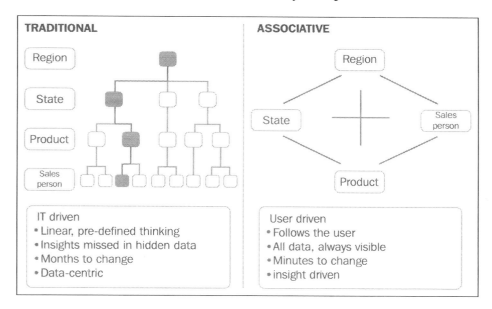

- Power of green, white, and grey: In a QlikView application, selected data elements are displayed in green, associated data is displayed in white, and non-associated data is shown in grey.

  All the data is always present.

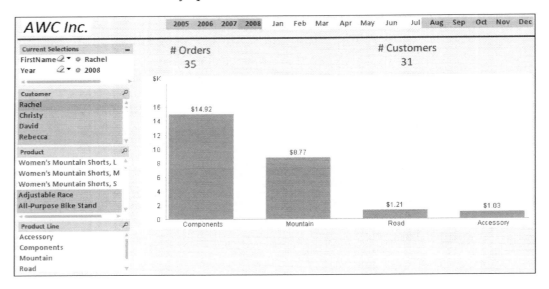

- A QlikView application development utilizes QlikView desktop. It involves, connecting to any format of data, extracting and transforming data by writing scripts, designing interactive dashboards by creating different visualization objects, and deploying applications on the server. Users access this application via access point.

- A QlikView design file has the extension .qvw. Qvw is also used to create QVD (QlikView data file). QVD stores the data extracted from the data source. You will learn about the power of QVDs in the subsequent chapters. A QlikView design file is referred to as qvw, document, or application, but they all mean the same.

Getting started

This book uses a data model based on Adventure works 2012 database.

Joe Smith is being hired as a QlikView consultant by Adventure Works Inc.. Adventure works has recently purchased QlikView. Their employees got an overview of QlikView, but they need help in enhancing their QlikView knowledge and implementing the QlikView dashboarding application.

This book will take you on a wonderful journey with Joe Smith and will provide you with QlikView essentials, which you will require as a successful QlikView consultant.

The development life cycle of QlikView implementations

Joe Smith, being a seasoned QlikView consultant, knows that for successful implementation he needs to follow the development life cycle of QlikView. At a high level, he will do the following:

- Gain an understanding of Adventure works' business
- Gather user requirements
- Analyze data model/data sources
- Follow data modeling best practices
- Load data
- Follow visualization/dashboarding best practices
- Create dashboard
- Deployment

About Adventure Works

Adventure Works Cycles, is a large, multinational manufacturing company. The company manufactures and sells metal and composite bicycles to North American, European, and Asian commercial markets.

Coming off a successful fiscal year, Adventure Works Cycles is looking to broaden its market share by targeting their sales to their best customers, extending their product availability through an external website, and reducing their cost of sales through lower production costs.

User requirements

At Adventure works, executive management wants to utilize QlikView to address the following:

- Create an enterprise wide, scalable Business Analytics platform where the information is easily available, shared, and collaborated
- Integrate data from different data sources
- Gain visibility into the company's key performance indicators
- Comparative analysis of data by different time periods

- Access relevant information quickly and efficiently
- Gain business insights to make better business decisions

Analyze data model/data sources

After understanding the business and business requirements, it's time to analyze the underlying data.

Adventure works is a relational database.

Management is interested in utilizing the data elements stored in the following tables. Tables are sourced from relational database, Excel files, and text files.

- Product
- ProductSubcategory
- Product Category
- Order Header
- Order Detail
- Customers
- Territory
- Employees
- Shippers

At high level, the tables from the source system have the following relationships:

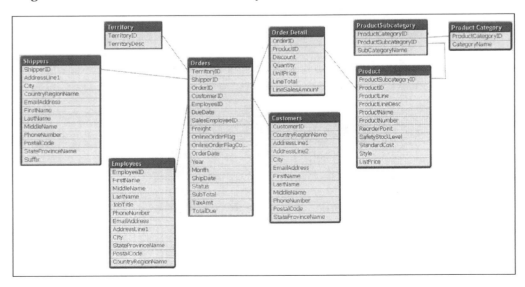

Star schema and snow flake schema

QlikView can handle Star schema and Snow flake schemas effectively. Star schema is simple to understand. It is good for reporting as number of joins are reduced.

Star schema consists of dimensions and facts. It has a fact in the middle and dimensions surrounding the fact. The schema shapes like a star and hence the name star schema.

- **Facts**: A fact table contains numeric value. It contains a quantitative value such as sales, revenue, or profit.
- **Dimensions**: A dimension table contains textual description. Dimensions provide context to the facts, for example, sales by product.

Fact tables contain foreign keys of dimension tables. The following schematic represents the relationship between the fact and dimension tables:

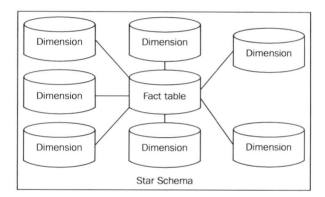

In a snow flake schema, a dimension is not connected directly to the fact. It is connected to another dimension.

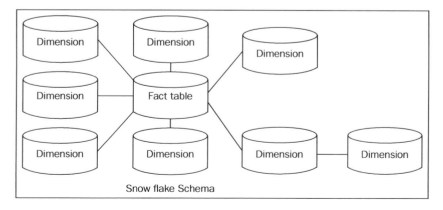

In Adventure works source data model, the dimension tables are:

- Customers
- Product
- ProductSubcategory
- Product Category
- Territory
- Employees

The fact tables are:

- Order Header
- Order Detail

QlikView development setup

To set up the QlikView development environment, download the code bundle for this book from Packt Publishing's website (http://www.packtpub.com/support) and then unzip the downloaded file in your C drive within a folder with the same name as the ZIP file (QlikViewEssentials). The unzipped folder (C:\QlikViewEssentials) should now contain the following folder structure in it:

- Apps: This folder contains the .qvw files. Any design file created in QlikView has .qvw extension. These files are referred as document, app, or qvw.
- Data: This folder contains data files required by the application. It includes the access database .mdb file. Also, it contains excel and text files. This folder also contains a subfolder Qvds to store QVDs.
- Images: This folder contains the images required by the application.
- Includes: This folder contains any files to be included in the application, for example, data connection.

Summary

This chapter familiarizes us with QlikView. You learned about the different components of QlikView and QlikView installation. You are now equipped to learn subsequent chapters by gaining knowledge about the fictitious data model of Adventure Works Inc. and learning about data modeling best practices.

In the next chapter, you will dive more into data modeling by loading data from disparate datasources. You will also learn about resolving synthetic keys. You will learn about various data transformation techniques. It will help you in becoming an expert QlikView developer.

2
Extract, Transform, and Load

The power of any application lies in its data structure. QlikView can design very useful and functional data models. QlikView can extract data from disparate data sources and associate them to present a single version of the truth. The power of QlikView's ETL (extract, transform, and load) functionality can help organizations in transforming data.

In this chapter, you will learn how to extract data from different sources and transform them to design a data model. This data model will be used in later chapters to create dashboards. This chapter will help you in mastering ETL scripting in QlikView.

In this chapter, we shall learn about:

- Scripting essentials
- Building data models by loading data from relational data sources, Excel, and text files
- Creating calculated fields in the tables
- Different techniques to resolve synthetic keys
- Resolving circular references
- Loading Inline tables
- Resident load
- Including files
- Using If statements

Configuring settings

Before loading data in QlikView, we need to set up the user preferences and document properties:

1. Open the QlikView desktop. From the **File** menu, select **New**.

2. Save this new file as `QlikViewEssentials.qvw` into your `QlikViewEssentials\Apps` folder.

3. From the **Settings** menu, select **User Preferences**. Under the **Save** tab, make sure the **After Reload** option is checked.

4. From the **Settings** menu, select **Document Properties**. Under the **General** tab, check **Generate Logfile**. This will generate a log file and will help in debugging.

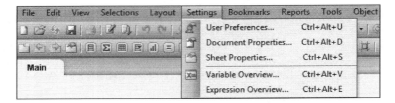

Scripting essentials

Scripting is a set of statements or commands that are written using a specific syntax. Script statements are executed to accomplish the desired results. In QlikView, scripts are written in the script editor. A script is written to load/extract data from data source tables and to transform data. Script uses QlikView specific and data source-specific functions. Script editor is invoked by pressing *Ctrl + E* or using the script editor icon ![icon] from the toolbar. Script editor will look like the following:

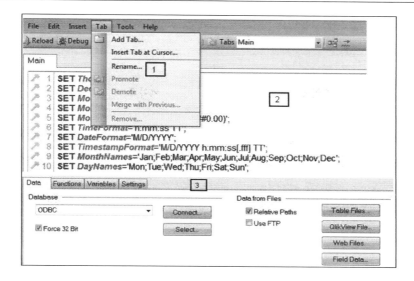

Here are some of the highlights of the script editor:

- Script statements can be organized by using tabs.
- The first tab is **Main** and it is created by default. This tab has certain variables already declared. These variables are set using your operating system settings.
- At the bottom of the script editor is a set of tabs used for loading data and script generation. Data is loaded from the **Data** tab and data from the files.
- The script is executed from left to right and top to bottom, with the exception being within specific load statements. Specific load statements are executed from bottom to top, as shown in the following image:

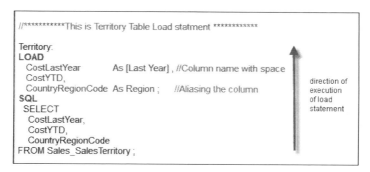

- Comments are given by using // or enclosing multiple lines between /*   */.

- Name should be given to a loaded table. This name will be used by QlikView when referencing the table. The table name should be suffixed by a colon ":".

- Field names can be aliased by using AS. If there is a space between the field name or table name then it should be enclosed by square brackets "[ ]".

- Table names and field names are case sensitive. "CostLastYear" is not the same as "costlastyear".

- All statements end with a semicolon ";".

- Execute script by clicking on the **Reload** icon ![Reload] on the toolbar.

- Use Table Viewer by pressing *Ctrl + T* to view the created data table and data model.

- Use the **Debug** option from the **File** menu to debug your script.

- View the log file for all the script execution steps. The log file is located in the same location as your QlikView document. The name of the log is the same as your QlikView document. So, in the case of QlikViewEssentials.qvw, it will be QlikViewEssentials.qvw.log.

One of the user requirements as discussed in *Chapter 1, QlikView Essentials*, is to integrate data from different sources. To accomplish this we will load data from different sources such as database tables, Excel, and text files. For database tables, you can see the structure of the table and data by using MS-Access. Your QlikViewEssentials/Data folder contains QlikViewEssentials.mdb, double click on this file and the database will open in MS-Access. MS-Access should be present on your machine to open this database. You can also open and view Excel and text files located in the QlikViewEssentials/Data folder and get familiarized with the data.

Connecting to the database

To load data from the database, we need to create a connection to the database:

1. Use the same QlikView file QlikViewEssentials.qvw that you created in the previous section.

2. Go to the **Main** tab. Data connections should be created in the **Main** tab, so that they can be available to all the tabs after the **Main** tab.

3. Open script editor as shown previously. On the **Data** tab, select **OLE DB** from the database drop-down list.

4. If you are working with a Windows 64-bit system, be sure to check **Force 32 Bit**.

5. Click the **Connect** button. In **Data Link Properties**, select **Microsoft Jet 4.0 OLE DB Provider** as you will be using the Access database, and click **Next**.

6. Browse to `QlikViewEssentials.mdb`, which is in the downloaded folder `QlikViewEssentials/Data`. Click on **Test Connection** to make sure the connection is correct.

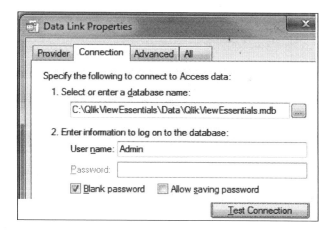

7. Connection to the database is successfully created.

```
OLEDB CONNECT32 TO [Provider=Microsoft Jet OLEDB 4.0;User ID=Admin;Data Source=C:\QlikViewEssentials\Data\QlikViewEssentials mdb;Mode=Share Deny None;Extended Properties="";
Jet OLEDB:System database="";
Jet OLEDB:Registry Path="";Jet OLEDB:Database Password="";Jet OLEDB:Engine Type=5;Jet OLEDB:Database Locking Mode=1;Jet OLEDB:Global Partial Bulk Ops=2;Jet OLEDB:Global Bulk Transactions=1;
Jet OLEDB:New Database Password="";Jet OLEDB:Create System Database=False;Jet OLEDB:Encrypt Database=False;Jet OLEDB:Don't Copy Locale on Compact=False;
Jet OLEDB:Compact Without Replica Repair=False;Jet OLEDB:SFP=False];
```

Loading the OrderHeader Table

The `OrderHeader` table is a database table. It stores details regarding the order such as order ID, order date, shipment details, and order amount. This table will help users in performing analysis at the order level such as orders related to customers, biggest sale by category, and so on:

1. From the **File** menu, open QlikView `QlikViewEssentials.qvw`, which you created in the earlier session.

2. Invoke script editor by clicking on the script editor icon  or by pressing *Ctrl + E*.

3. Create a new tab and name it `Orders`.

Add a new tab

4. From the **Data** tab, make sure the **Force 32 Bit** checkbox is checked and click on the **Select** button [Select..].

5. From **Database Tables**, select **OrderHeader**. Select all the fields or specific fields in the **Fields** section.

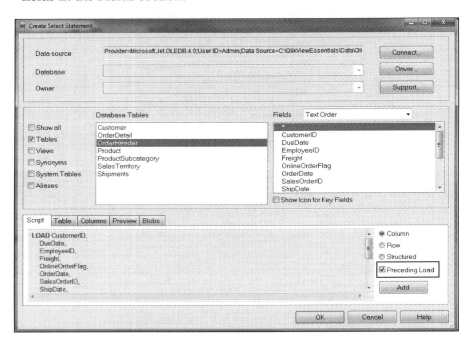

6. Make sure to check the **Preceding Load** at the bottom of the dialog box. Preceding load allows the use of QlikView functions within the Load statement.

You can load the table by unchecking **Preceding Load**. Without Preceding Load, you can only use vendor-specific functions. For example, if you use the Oracle database, you can use Oracle functions. Use of Preceding Load allows you to use QlikView functions. Preceding Load is also used for data transformations.

7. Click **OK**.

8. Provide a comment on your script to show that this is the Orders table load script.

9. Give the name of the table as Orders.

10. The load script will appear as follows:

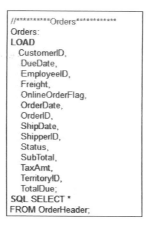

```
//**********Orders***********
Orders:
LOAD
  CustomerID,
    DueDate,
    EmployeeID,
    Freight,
    OnlineOrderFlag,
    OrderDate,
    OrderID,
    ShipDate,
    ShipperID,
    Status,
    SubTotal,
    TaxAmt,
    TerritoryID,
    TotalDue;
SQL SELECT *
FROM OrderHeader;
```

11. To execute the script, click on the reload icon ⟳Reload from the toolbar or press *Ctrl + R*.

12. After script execution, the **Sheet Properties** dialog box appears. This shows the fields loaded in the QlikView document. It also displays the system fields generated. System fields are the fields that are prefixed by "$", for example, `$Field`.

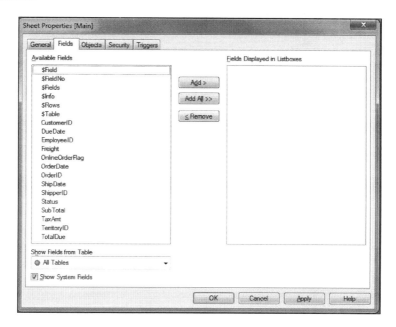

With the help of system fields you can understand the complete structure of the application. You can display these fields in list boxes or table boxes for ease of analysis.

Loading the OrderDetail table

In this exercise we will load the OrderDetail table. OrderDetail is a database table.

The OrderDetail table contains the details of the orders stored in the OrderHeader table. It stores information regarding the products ordered by the customer. One order may contain multiple products:

1. Invoke script editor by clicking on the script editor icon 📝 or by pressing *Ctrl + E.*

2. Go to the Orders tab. Place the cursor on an empty row after the previously loaded Order table.

3. From the **Data** tab, click on the **Select** button [Select...].

4. From the database tables, select the OrderDetail table.

5. Provide a comment to show that this is an OrderDetail load script and give the name of the table as [Order Detail].

6. Your script for OrderDetail will appear as follows:

```
//**********Orders Details***********
[Order Detail]:
LOAD
    Discount,
    OrderID,
    OrderQty,
    ProductID,
    UnitPrice;
SQL SELECT *
FROM OrderDetail;
```

7. Save your script.

8. To execute script, click on the reload icon 🔄 Reload from the toolbar or press *Ctrl + R.*

9. From the **File** menu, click on the **Table Viewer** icon 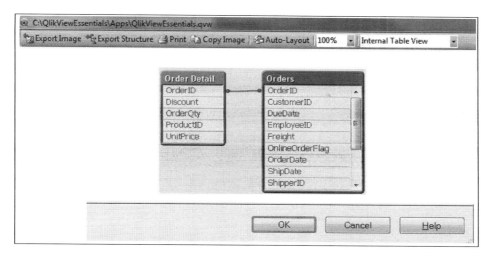 or press *Ctrl + T*. In table viewer you can see how loaded tables are connected.

10. Observe that the `Orders` and `Order Detail` tables are connected based on the `OrderID` field. QlikView associates two tables based on common fields between the two tables.

Creating fields in the Order table

It is sometimes necessary to create fields in the loaded tables as these fields may not be present in your source table. It is easy to create fields in QlikView tables. We will create fields for year and month as these fields are not present in the source tables. Year and month fields will be important to perform year-by-year comparisons or to see the data by year and month:

1. Open the script editor by pressing *Ctrl + E*.

2. Go to the **Orders** tab.

3. Locate `OrderDate` and add the following lines anywhere in the load statement for Order using OrderDate. Remember field names are case sensitive:

```
Year (OrderDate) As Year,
Month (OrderDate) As Month,
```

4. Similarly, add a calculation in the `Order Detail` table for LineTotal. Locate `Order Detail` load script in the **Orders** tab and add the following code:

```
UnitPrice * OrderQty As LineTotal
```

5. Add the calculation for `LinesSalesAmount` in the `Order Detail` table using Preceding Load. Preceding Load takes input from the previous load statement. It allows you to define multiple transformations and calculations within one load script.

6. Add the following code on top of the `Order Detail` load script:

```
LOAD *,
LineTotal  *  (1-Discount) As LineSalesAmount;
```

7. This load statement takes `LineTotal` from the previous load statement and uses it to calculate `LineSalesAmount`.

8. Alias `OrderQty` to make it a more business-friendly name:

```
OrderQty As Quantity,
```

9. After performing the above transformation, your load script will appear as follows:

```
1
2   //**********Orders**********
3   Orders:
4   LOAD
5       CustomerID,
6       DueDate,
7       EmployeeID,
8       Freight,
9       OnlineOrderFlag,
10      OrderDate,
11      Year(OrderDate) As Year,
12      Month(OrderDate) As Month,
13      OrderID,
14      ShipDate,
15      ShipperID,
16      Status,
17      SubTotal,
18      TaxAmt,
19      TerritoryID,
20      TotalDue;
21  SQL SELECT *
22  FROM OrderHeader;
23
24  //**********Orders Details**********
25  [Order Detail]:
26  LOAD *,                              // This will ensure that all the columns from the previous load are loaded
27  LineTotal  * (1-Discount) As LineSalesAmount; //Preceding load. Takes LineTotal from the previous load statement
28  LOAD
29      Discount,
30      OrderID,
31      OrderQty          As Quantity,
32      ProductID,
33      UnitPrice,
34      UnitPrice * OrderQty As LineTotal ;
35  SQL SELECT *
36  FROM OrderDetail;
37
```

Loading the Customer table

In this exercise we will load Customer table. Customer is a database table. Customer tables store the details about the customers. These are the customers who have ordered the products:

1. Invoke script editor by clicking on the script editor icon ✍ or by pressing *Ctrl + E.*

2. Create a new tab by clicking on 🗂 and name it Dimensions.

   Organizing script statements using tabs is helpful in understanding and debugging the code. As Customer table is a Dimension table, the load script of Customer is written in a new tab.

3. Click on **Select** and choose **Customer** in **Database Tables**. Click on **OK**.

4. Provide a comment and give the table name as Customers.

5. Reload the script.

6. From the file menu, click on the Table Viewer icon ▦ or press *Ctrl + T* to examine the data model.

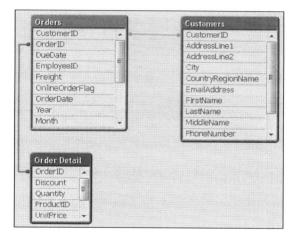

Loading the Product table

In this exercise we will load the Product table. Product is a database table. The Product table contains the information about the product. The Order Details table refers to this table. The products ordered by the customers are stored in this table.

1. Invoke script editor by clicking on the script editor icon ✍ or by pressing *Ctrl + E.*

2. Go to the **Dimensions** tab and place your cursor in the empty space below the Customer load script.

3. Click on the **Select** button and select **Product** table from the **Database Tables** list.

4. Provide a comment and name the table as Product.

5. Reload.

6. Press *Ctrl + T* to view the Table Viewer.

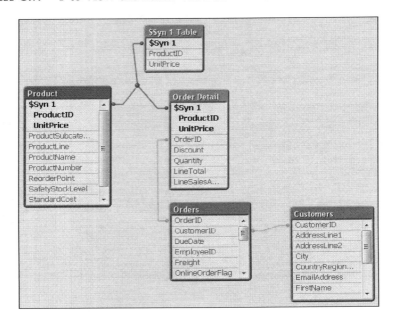

Resolving the synthetic keys

Observe the previous screenshot of the Table Viewer, which shows the creation of synthetic keys. Synthetic keys are created due to the presence of multiple common columns across multiple tables. This may cause QlikView to use complex keys to create connections in the data model.

Synthetic keys are generally resource intensive, and make the data model complex and hard to understand. In QlikView, the association between two tables should be made based on a single common column between the two tables. *Synthetic keys should always be eliminated.*

How to resolve synthetic keys

Synthetic keys can be removed by:

- Removing the fields that do not provide context to the data model
- Renaming the fields
- By using the `Qualify` statement

Removing synthetic keys between the Product and Order Detail tables

1. In the previous data model, you can see the connection between the tables is made on two columns: `ProductID` and `UnitPrice`.

2. `UnitPrice` in the `Product` table is different from the `UnitPrice` in the `OrderDetail` table. `UnitPrice` in the `Product` table is the "list price of the product" whereas the `UnitPrice` in the `OrderDetail` table is the "product-unit price for the specific order". Therefore, we can rename the `UnitPrice` in the `Product` table.

3. Open Script Editor. Navigate to the `Product` table in the **Dimensions** tab.

4. Rename `UnitPrice` in `Product` table to `ListPrice` by using the following:

```
UnitPrice As ListPrice
```

5. Save and reload your script and open the Table Viewer.

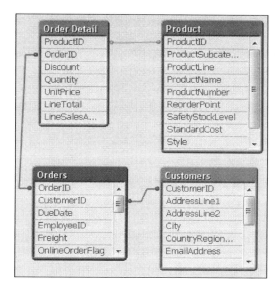

Loading the ProductSubcategory table

1. Invoke script editor by clicking on the script editor icon [image] or by pressing *Ctrl + E*.

2. Go to the **Dimensions** tab and place your cursor in the empty space below the Product load script.

3. Click on the **Select** button and select **ProductSubcategory** table from the **Database Tables** list.

4. Provide a comment and table name.

5. Reload.

Loading data from text and Excel files

QlikView can load delimited text files, fixed record files, DIF files, Excel files, HTML files, and XML files. These file types are referred as "table files" in QlikView.

In our source data, we have some data stored in text and Excel files.

Loading the Product Category table

In this exercise, we will load the Product Category table. The data for Product Category is present in a text file:

1. Use the same QlikView file QlikViewEssentials.qvw, which you created in the previous section.

2. Invoke the script editor.

3. Navigate to the **Dimensions** tab and go to the empty space below the previously loaded table.

4. At the bottom of script editor, in **Data from Files** group, make sure **Relative Paths** is checked.

The path to a file can be an absolute or a relative path. The absolute path for the `ProductCategory` file is `C:\QlikViewEssentials\Data\ProductCategory.txt`. If you move your application to a different machine, and the location of the `ProductCategory` file is on a different drive other than `C:`, then your load statement will fail as it will not find the file.

A relative path, on the other hand, specifies the location of a directory relative to the current directory. A relative path will be useful when you move your application to a different machine. The relative path of `ProductCategory.txt` is `..\Data\ProductCategory.txt` and it will still remain valid as long as the file resides in this path, irrespective of which drive is used.

5. In the **Data from Files** group, click on the **Table Files** button [Table Files...].

6. Browse and open `ProductCategory.txt`. This file is in the downloaded folder, under `QlikViewEssentials\Data`.

7. Verify the settings in the file wizard.

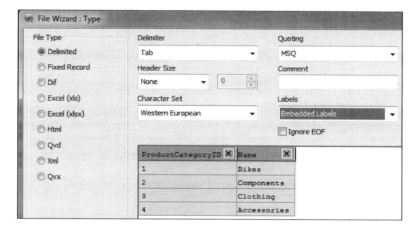

8. Using table files, you can load various file types as listed on the left, under **File Type**. A text file is a delimited file. It can be delimited by a tab, semicolon, or comma. Select the delimiter based on your file. For **Labels**, if the column headers in your file are stored in the first line of the file, specify **Embedded Labels**. Column headers can be explicitly specified. In such scenarios, specify **Explicit** under **Labels**.

9. The load script for `Product Category` should look like the following:

```
//**********ProductCategory************
[Product Category]:
LOAD
    ProductCategoryID,
    CategoryName
FROM
[..\Data\ProductCategory.txt]
(txt, codepage is 1252, embedded labels, delimiter is '\t', msq);
```

Loading Employee.xlsx

Employee data is in Microsoft Excel format. We will follow the steps to load Excel files using the **Table Files** option. `Employee.xlsx` contains the details about the Adventure Works employees. Some of these employees are also sales persons. Here, our objective is to load employee details and, later in the exercise, we will use this table to identify sales persons.

1. Invoke script editor if it is not already open.
2. Create a new tab and name it `Employees`.

Add a new tab

3. At the bottom of script editor, in **Data from Files** group, make sure **Relative Paths** is checked.
4. Click on the **Table Files** button ⬚ Table Files... .
5. Browse and open `Employee.xlsx`. This file is in the downloaded folder, under `QlikViewEssentials\Data`.
6. Verify the selections in the **File Type** wizard:
   - **File Type**: **Excel (xlsx)**.
   - **Tables**: **Employee**. If you have multiple worksheets in your Excel, you will see those worksheets in the drop-down menu.
   - **Header Size**: **None**. This is used when Excel has a different header size.
   - **Labels**: **Embedded Labels**. This is used to configure the headers in your Excel.

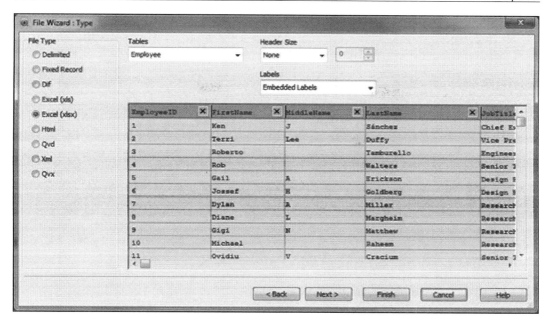

7. Click **Finish** to return to the **Employees** tab and load the script.

8. Observe the generated load statement.

9. Provide a comment to the script as `Employees` table.

10. Remove the directory; give a name to your table as `Employees`.

11. Load the data by clicking on the reload icon 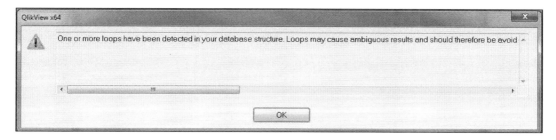 from the toolbar. As you load the data, you will get a warning, as follows:

12. Invoke Table Viewer by clicking on 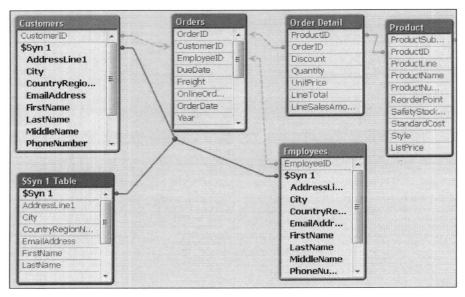 or by pressing *Ctrl + T*. You will see the following picture in the data model:

Circular reference in data model

Circular reference and loosely coupled tables

The previous warning and data model brings us to the discussion of circular reference and loosely coupled tables.

Circular reference

Circular reference, or loop, occurs when more than one path exists between the tables. In the previous example, there are two paths to the Orders table. One through Customer table, and the other through Employees table. This loop may occur in ambiguous results.

Loosely coupled tables

QlikView handles this scenario automatically by setting one or more tables as loosely coupled. This is often a transaction table.

If you navigate to **Settings | Document Properties**, under the **Tables** tab, you will see the `Orders` table as a **Loosely Coupled** table. If you want to change the default behavior of QlikView, you can either change the **Loosely Coupled** table in the document properties or use loosely coupled statement in the script. Loosely coupled tables will show dotted lines in the Table Viewer.

This circular reference is occurring due to connections from `Orders` to `Customers` to `Syn` table to `Employees` and back to `Orders`.

Resolving circular reference

Resolving circular reference removes the ambiguity in the data model:

1. If we go back to the Table Viewer model, we see that there is a synthetic key due to the presence of more than one common column between **Customers** and **Employees**.

2. Note that FirstName, LastName, **CountryRegionName**, **City**, and other fields in the **Customers** and **Employees** column will be different.

3. Rename the common columns in `Employees` table. The load script of `Employees` table should appear as follows:

```
//**********Employee***********
Employees:
LOAD
  EmployeeID,
  FirstName              As [Emp FirstName],
  MiddleName             As [Emp MiddleName],
  LastName               As [Emp LastName],
  JobTitle,
  PhoneNumber            As [Emp PhoneNumber],
  EmailAddress           As [Emp Email Address],
  AddressLine1           As [Emp Address],
  City                   As [Emp City],
  StateProvinceName      As [Emp State],
  PostalCode             As [Emp PostalCode],
  CountryRegionName      As [Emp Country]
FROM
[..\Data\Employees.xlsx] (ooxml, embedded labels, table is Employee);
```

 Alternatively, all the columns in a table can be renamed using the `Qualify` statement. The `Qualify` statement qualifies the column name with the table name. The `Qualify` statement is explained in detail later in the chapter.

4. This should eliminate the circular loop. You can see the model in the Table Viewer.

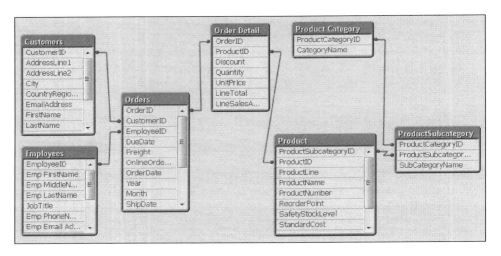

Loading the SalesTerritory and Shipment tables

The SalesTerritory table contains the territory details. This table connects with OrderHeader table. The Shipment table stores details about the shipper responsible for shipping the ordered product:

1. From the **File** menu, open QlikViewEssentials.qvw, which you created in the earlier session.

2. Invoke script editor by clicking on the script editor icon ![icon] or by pressing *Ctrl + E.*

3. Navigate to the **Dimensions** tab and go to empty space after the last loaded table.

4. Click on the **Select** button and select **SalesTerritory** table from the **Database Tables** list.

5. Provide a comment and name the table Territory.

Loading an Inline table

Inline load is used if data is to be typed within the script and not loaded from a file. The Inline data wizard is also used to create inline load.

Inline load is used when the source database does not contain the columns you need for your application.

We will create an Inline table to load the country and region. Since we want these regions to be associated with a customer's country, we will use CountryRegionName:

1. Use the same QlikView file QlikViewEssentials.qvw that you created in the previous section.

2. Invoke script editor and create a new tab Inline.

3. From the menu, use **Insert | Load Statement** and select **Load Inline**.

4. The **Inline Data** wizard will appear, which is similar to Excel but you cannot perform calculations here as in Excel.

5. Double click on *F1* in the wizard to type the first column name as CountyRegionName. Double click on the second column to enter the second column name as Region. These are the two column names of your table.

6. Now insert values for these columns.

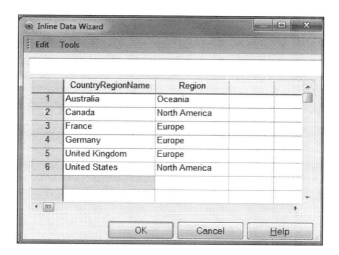

7. Click **OK**. Your inline load script will be generated. Give it a table name.

8. Your inline load will appear as follows:

```
CountryRegion_Inline:
LOAD * INLINE [
    CountryRegionName, Region
    Australia, Oceania
    Canada, North America
    France, Europe
    Germany, Europe
    United Kingdom, Europe
    United States, North America
];
```

9. Since the first column is CountryRegionName, it will get associated with Customers table.

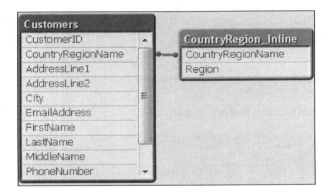

The Qualify statement

The Qualify statement is another way to resolve synthetic keys. It is a method to rename a column. It qualifies a column with a table name. It is similar to Tablename and Fieldname used in SQL. It is a faster method of aliasing a column, if multiple columns need to be renamed to avoid synthetic keys or loops. Qualify continues till it hits an Unqualify statement:

```
Syntax :
Qualify * ;
...
...
...
UnQualify * ;
```

Loading the Shippers table

We will use Qualify while loading the Shippers table because it contains fields that are common with other tables. If these fields are not renamed then it will create synthetic keys. Qualify will rename all the fields in the table. In this exercise, we will see why Qualify is used:

1. Invoke the script editor by pressing *Ctrl + E*.

2. Navigate to the **Dimensions** tab and go to the empty space below the previously loaded table.

3. Click on the **Select** button and select the **Shippers** table.

   Your load script will appear as follows:

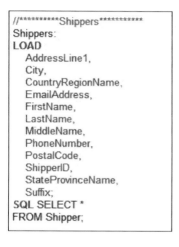

```
//**********Shippers***********
Shippers:
LOAD
    AddressLine1,
    City,
    CountryRegionName,
    EmailAddress,
    FirstName,
    LastName,
    MiddleName,
    PhoneNumber,
    PostalCode,
    ShipperID,
    StateProvinceName,
    Suffix;
SQL SELECT *
FROM Shipper;
```

4. Reload the script. You will get a warning for loop, and synthetic keys will be created. This happened since the Shippers and Customers tables have more than one common field, for example, FirstName, LastName, and MiddleName.

5. You can resolve this loop and synthetic key by renaming columns in the Shippers table. Rename columns using the Qualify statement. Since ShipperID is used to join with Orders table, make sure to unqualify ShipperID.

6. Make sure to have the last statement as Unqualify otherwise it will qualify all the load scripts after this load statement.

7. Your modified script will appear as follows:

```
QUALIFY *;
UNQUALIFY ShipperID;
//**********Shippers**********
Shippers:
LOAD
    AddressLine1,
    City,
    CountryRegionName,
    EmailAddress,
    FirstName,
    LastName,
    MiddleName,
    PhoneNumber,
    PostalCode,
    ShipperID,
    StateProvinceName,
    Suffix;
SQL SELECT *
FROM Shipper;
UNQUALIFY *;
```

A word about resident load and Exists

Resident load is used to load a table that is already loaded in the QlikView document. Resident load can be used to create a new table or additional transformation.

Exists (field, expression) is used to determine whether the specific field value exists in the loaded fields so far.

*   Field is a name or a string expression evaluating to a field name.

*   Expression is a valid expression that results in the value to be compared in the specified field. If omitted, the current record's value in the specified field will be assumed. For example, `Exists (Country, 'England')` returns -1 (true) if the field value `'England'` is found in the current content of the field `Country`.

Finding the sales person

Now, we will work on the problem of identifying the Sales Person who sold the Orders. This will be done using the Resident load and Exists clause.

We can assume that the sales person will be an employee of the company. The sales person is an employee but not all employees are sales persons. The objective here is to identify sales persons among the list of employees in the Employee table:

1. Open the QlikView document QlikViewEssentials.qvw that has been used so far.

2. From the **File** menu, select **Edit Script** or press *Ctrl + E*.

3. Go to the **Orders** Tab. Navigate to Orders' load script. Use EmployeeID to create a new field for SalesEmployeeID. This field will be used to identify the sales person in the Orders table:

    ```
    EmployeeID As SalesEmployeeID,
    ```

4. Navigate to the **Employees** tab. Go to the empty space after the Employees data load. We will create the SalesPerson table by using the fields of the Employees table.

5. The SalesPerson table load script will appear like the following:

```
SalesPerson:
Load
    EmployeeID,
    [Emp FirstName] & ' ' & [Emp LastName] As [SalesPerson Name], //String concatenation to create SalesPerson Name
    JobTitle As SalesPersonTitle
Resident Employees                              // Used to load the fields from previous loaded Employees table
where Exists(SalesEmployeeID,EmployeeID);       //Loading the EmployeeID which exist in the Orders table
```

Using If statements in the script

If-then-else is used to control the execution path of the script based on one or multiple conditions.

The If statement in QlikView uses the following syntax:

```
If (condition, then, else)
```

If the condition is true, the then part is processed. If the condition is false, the else portion is processed.

We will use If statements to group ProductLine:

1. Invoke script editor.

2. Navigate to the **Dimensions** tab and go to load script of Product table.

3. Write the following line of code anywhere in the `Product` table:

```
if(ProductLine = 'M','Mountain',
  if(ProductLine = 'R','Road',
  if(ProductLine = 'S', 'Accessory', 'Components')) )
  As ProductLineDesc,
```

4. Reload your script and make sure `ProductLineDesc` has the correct values.

Including files using the Include statement

In order to share a snippet of code or data, use the `Include` statement. A file can be shared across applications using `Include`.

A good use case is a database connection string. You can store a database connection string in the text file and it can be included in any number of QlikView applications. In case the connection string changes, you need to just change one text file.

In this exercise we will keep the database connection string in the text file and use the `Include` statement to include it in the script:

1. Invoke the script editor and go to the **Main** tab.
2. Copy the OLEDB32 connection string and comment on the connection string.
3. Paste this connect string into a text file and name this file as `DBConnection.txt`.
4. Save `DBConnection.txt` in your `Includes` folder under the following `C:\QlikViewEssentials\Includes`.
5. Go to script editor and navigate to the **Main** tab. From the menu, choose **Insert | Include Statement**.
6. Browse to your `Includes` folder and open `DBConnection.txt`.
7. Your include statement will look like the following:

```
$(Include=..\includes\dbconnection.txt);
```

8. Save and reload your file. Now your connection string is coming from this file.

More on Table Viewer

Table Viewer is used to view tables loaded in the QlikView document. On the top of the Table Viewer you can see two options: **Internal Table View** and **Source Table View**.

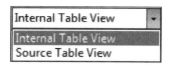

Internal Table View shows the data tables as QlikView stores them. **Source Table View** shows data tables as QlikView reads them.

If you hover the cursor over a table header, it will display the table name, number of rows loaded, and number of keys in the table:

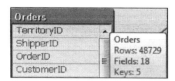

If you place your cursor on one of the key fields, some more information is displayed:

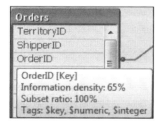

As seen in the preceding screenshot, the following information is displayed:

- **Information density** displays the number of records that are not null.
- **Subset ratio** is the number of distinct values of this field found in this table as compared to the total number of distinct values of this field (for example, other tables also).
- **Tags** display the tags added in the script or the system tags.

Use this information to perform a high-level check of your data model.

Time to review your data model so far

In the previous exercises, we have loaded the data source tables. These tables will be used in creating visualizations. It is important that tables are connected correctly, and synthetic keys and loops are resolved. Review the following tables we have loaded so far.

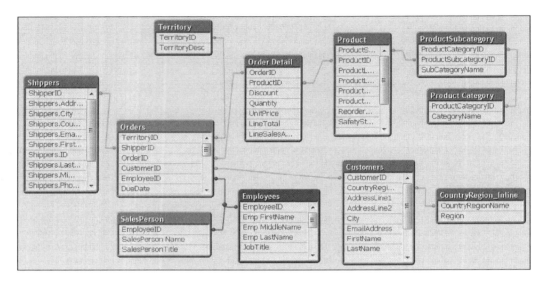

Summary

This chapter covered the basics of QlikView scripting and data loads. You were able to load data from a relational database and flat files to get started on creating a data model. This chapter also covered the data transformations required to find a sales person, ProductLine grouping, and calculated fields in the tables. As more tables are loaded, synthetic and circular loops are produced. By learning to resolve synthetic keys and loops, you are on your way to producing an optimized data model.

In the next chapter, you will learn how to reduce the number of tables and joins in your data model by using mapping load and applymap functions. You will also learn about different kind of joins in QlikView.

Optimizing Your Data Model

3

Your data model should always be simple and easy to understand. An expert data modeler will always clean up the data model to remove any unnecessary tables.

QlikView provides different techniques for data model cleanup. In this chapter we will learn ways to clean up the data model and create a star schema.

In this chapter we shall:

- Learn about mapping tables and mapping load
- Clean up the data model using "mapping load" and "apply map"
- Learn about different kinds of joins
- Aggregate data
- Learn to use "concatenate"

Let's review the data model that we created in the last chapter:

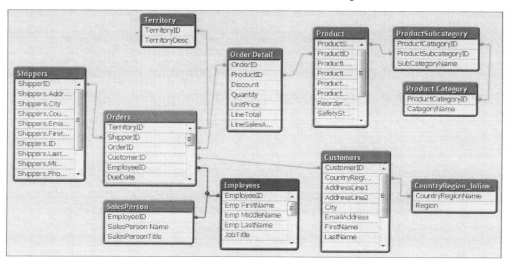

One of our requirements is to create a robust data model that is clean, easy to understand, and helps in data analysis. This chapter describes techniques to achieve this requirement. By understanding and applying the concepts of mapping load, concatenate, and joins, we can create a more useful data model.

Mapping table essentials

Mapping tables are very useful in QlikView data modeling. Some of the uses of mapping tables include data cleansing, renaming the data source-specific column names with business-friendly names, and providing comments in the script. The following points discuss some of the components and properties of mapping tables:

- Mapping load is used to reduce the number of tables in a data model. Mapping prefix is used to create a mapping table. Mapping tables are used only for field mapping and are automatically dropped after script execution.

- These are usually the look-up tables.

- Mapping tables must have two columns. Even if the table has more columns, you can use only two columns at a time to achieve mapping table functionality. The same table can be used multiple times in case other columns need to be mapped.

- The first column is always a key (ID) column. The second column contains the desired mapping value. The first column field name can differ between the mapping table and the mapped table.

- Use the `ApplyMap` function in the table to compare the key/ID field to get the desired mapping value.

- It provides a third optional parameter when no comparison is found.

Looking at the previous data model, you can identify the tables that are good candidates for mapping load. These tables will be:

- `Territory`
- `ProductSubcategory`
- `Product Category`
- `CountryRegion_Inline`

Mapping load – Territory table

The objective here is to add `TerritoryDesc` to the `Orders` table and remove the `Territory` table from the data model. This will help in data model cleanup as one table will be reduced:

1. As a best practice, all mapping loads should be in one tab. This tab should be the very first tab in the script after the **Main** tab.

2. Open the QlikView file `QlikViewEssentials.qvw` that you have been using so far. Save as `QlikViewEssentials_Chap3.qvw`.

3. Invoke the script editor by pressing *Ctrl + E*.

4. Create a new tab and name it `Mapping`. Move this tab all the way to the left by using the Promote Tab icon as highlighted in the following screenshot. It should be your tab after the **Main** tab.

5. Navigate to the **Dimensions** tab and cut the load script of `SalesTerritory` and paste it in the **Mapping** tab.

6. Navigate to the **Mapping** tab, change the comment, and name the table as `Territory_Map`.

7. Prefix the load statement with the `Mapping` keyword. This will treat the `SalesTerritory` table as a mapping table. This table will not be present in the memory and will get dropped after the script execution.

8. Make the first column as the ID column and name it `TerriID`, and name the second column as `TerriDesc`. Names are optional.

9. The mapping table load script should look like the following:

```
//*********Sales Territory Map***********
Territory_Map:
Mapping LOAD
        TerritoryID     As TerriID,
        TerritoryDesc As TerriDesc;
SQL SELECT *
FROM SalesTerritory;
```

10. Navigate to the **Orders** tab, and go to the last line in the `Orders` table load statement after `TotalDue`. Add "," after `TotalDue`. Use the `ApplyMap` function to add a `TerritoryDesc` column in the `Orders` table. Name this column as `[Order Territory]`.

    `ApplyMap('Territory_Map',TerritoryID,'Territory Not Found') As [Order Territory]`

    This is the `ApplyMap` syntax. Here, `Territory_Map` is the name of the mapping table. `TerritoryID` is the lookup column. `'Territory Not Found'` is an optional parameter in case the match is not found.

11. Your `Orders` table script should look like the following:

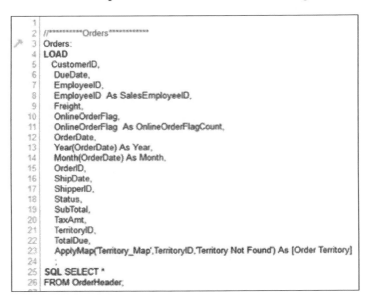

```
 1
 2  //***********Orders***********
 3  Orders:
 4  LOAD
 5      CustomerID,
 6      DueDate,
 7      EmployeeID,
 8      EmployeeID As SalesEmployeeID,
 9      Freight,
10      OnlineOrderFlag,
11      OnlineOrderFlag As OnlineOrderFlagCount,
12      OrderDate,
13      Year(OrderDate) As Year,
14      Month(OrderDate) As Month,
15      OrderID,
16      ShipDate,
17      ShipperID,
18      Status,
19      SubTotal,
20      TaxAmt,
21      TerritoryID,
22      TotalDue,
23      ApplyMap('Territory_Map',TerritoryID,'Territory Not Found') As [Order Territory]
24      ;
25  SQL SELECT *
26  FROM OrderHeader;
```

12. Reload your script.

13. Navigate to Table Viewer (*Ctrl + T*) .You will notice that the `Territory` table has gone and the `Order Territory` column has been added to the `Orders` table.

14. Create a list box for `Order Territory`.

15. To create a list box, close the script editor by clicking **OK**. Anywhere in the empty space on the sheet, right click and choose **New Sheet Object** and select **List Box**. In the properties of the list box, select **Order Territory** under the **Field** section.

You will see a new field is being created. Notice `Territory Not Found` because in some cases no match is found between the two tables.

Mapping load – Product Category and ProductSubcategory tables

Here the objective is to add the [Category Desc] to the `ProductSubcategory` table and then we will add Category desc and subcategory name from the `ProductSubcategory` table to the `Product` table:

1. Open `QlikViewEssentials_Chap3.qvw`.

2. Invoke the script editor by pressing *Ctrl + E*.

3. Navigate to the **Dimensions** tab and cut the `Product Category` load script and paste it in the **Mapping** tab.

4. The mapping load of `Product Category` will appear as follows:

```
//**********Category Map***********
Category_Map:
 Mapping LOAD
    ProductCategoryID  As CategoryID,
    CategoryName       As CategoryName
FROM
[..\Data\ProductCategory.txt]
(txt, codepage is 1252, embedded labels, delimiter is '\t', msq);
```

5. Navigate to the **Dimensions** tab. Go to the last line of the ProductSubCategory load script and use ApplyMap to add [Category Desc] to the ProductSubcategory.

```
//**********ProductSubCategory***********
ProductSubCategory:
LOAD
    ProductCategoryID,
    ProductSubcategoryID,
    SubCategoryName,
    ApplyMap('Category_Map',ProductCategoryID,'N/A') As [Category Desc];
SQL SELECT *
FROM ProductSubcategory;
```

6. Save and execute your script. Review your data model in Table Viewer to see that the Product Category table is removed and Category Desc is added to the ProductSubcategory table.

Mapping load – ProductSubcategory table

Use mapping load with the ProductSubcategory table to get the subcategory name:

1. Navigate to the **Dimensions** tab and cut the ProductSubcategory load script and paste it in the **Mapping** tab.

2. The mapping load of ProductSubcategory for SubCategoryName and [Category Desc] will appear as follows:

```
//**********SubCategory Name Map***********
SubCategory_Map:
Mapping LOAD
    ProductSubcategoryID,
    SubCategoryName;
SQL SELECT *
FROM ProductSubcategory;

//**********SubCategory Category Desc Map***********
SubCategory_CategoryMap:
Mapping LOAD
    ProductSubcategoryID ,
    ApplyMap('Category_Map',ProductSubcategoryID,'No Category')  ;
SQL SELECT *
FROM ProductSubcategory;
```

3. Navigate to the **Dimensions** tab and go to the last line of the Product load script. Use ApplyMap to add SubCategoryName and CategoryName to the Product table. ApplyMap statements in the Product table will appear as follows:

```
ApplyMap('SubCategory_Map',ProductSubcategoryID,'No SubCategory')        As [SubCategory Desc],
ApplyMap('SubCategory_CategoryMap',ProductSubcategoryID,'No Category')  As  [Category Desc];
```

4. Save and load the script. View your data model in Table Viewer. The ProductSubcategory table is removed and SubCategoryName and CategoryName is added to the Product table.

Mapping load – CountryRegion_Inline

Use mapping load to get the CountryRegion_Desc from CountryRegion_Inline and include it in the Customers table:

1. The CountryRegion_Inline table can also be converted to the mapping table.

2. Navigate to the **Inline** tab and cut the CountryRegion_Inline load script and paste it in the **Mapping** tab.

3. The mapping load script for CountryRegion will appear as follows:

```
//***********CountryRegion Inline Map************
CountryRegion_Inline_Map:
Mapping LOAD * INLINE [
    CountryRegionName, Region
    Australia, Oceania
    Canada, North America
    France, Europe
    Germany, Europe
    United Kingdom, Europe
    United States, North America
];
```

4. Navigate to the **Dimensions** tab. Go to the load script of the Customers table and, in the last line, use ApplyMap as follows:

```
ApplyMap('CountryRegion_Inline_Map',CountryRegionName,'N/A') As CountryRegionDesc;
```

5. Save and load the script.

6. Review the data model in Table Viewer. The data model so far will appear as follows. It is much cleaner with fewer tables.

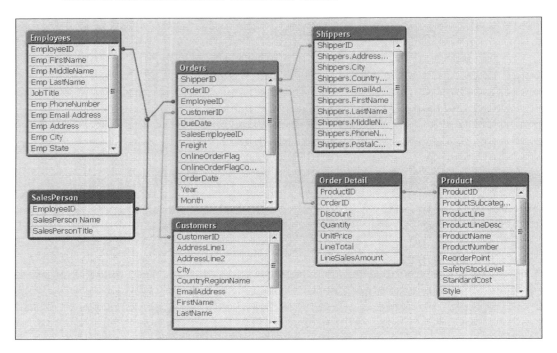

Concatenation

Another way to optimize your data model in QlikView is through concatenation.

Concatenation is a way to combine or merge tables. It is similar to Union All in SQL. It appends rows from one table to another. The result of concatenation between two tables (Table1 and Table2, for example) is that a new table contains the sum of the numbers of records in Table1 and Table2. Concatenate is used when you have two fact tables in your data model. Two fact tables are not good for your data model. You can combine them using concatenate or link tables. Link tables are explained in the next chapter.

Concatenate is also useful when you have to combine two tables with similar structures. Say, for example, your organization has an Employee table that stores employee data. Your organization buys another company and now wants to merge the details of the employees of this new company with the existing Employee table.

Let's explore different concatenation options:

- **Automatic concatenation**: If the field names and the number of fields in two or more tables are exactly the same, QlikView will automatically concatenate the output of the different load statements into one table.
- **Forced concatenation**: If the field names and the number of fields in two or more tables are NOT exactly the same, QlikView will allow you to force concatenation by the use of Concatenate keyword.
- **No concatenate**: If the field names and the number of fields in two or more tables are exactly the same, QlikView will automatically concatenate them but you can avoid such automatic concatenation by using the NoConcatenate keyword.

Concatenation example

Create an Inline table in QlikView to understand the concept of concatenation:

Automatic Concatenation

1. Navigate to the **Inline** tab.
2. Create two Inline tables as shown in the following:

```
//Concatenate example
Table1:
Load * Inline [
col1,col2
a,b
c,d
e,f
];

Table2:
Load * Inline [
col1,col2
a,b
c,d
e,f
];
```

3. Save and reload the script.
4. View the data model in Table Viewer. You will see only one table with six rows. This is because Table2 automatically concatenated with Table1.

NoConcatenate

Use the same script and add NoConcatenate between the two load scripts:

In Table View you will see two tables, Table1 and Table2. You will see that the synthetic key between them, as column names in the tables, are the same.

Forced concatenation

To test force concatenation, comment the previous Table1 and Table2 load scripts.

1. Now create two tables with different columns and use the Concatenate keyword to force concatenation.

```
//Force Concatenate example
Table1:
Load * Inline [
col1,col2
a,b
c,d
e,f
];
Concatenate
Table2:
Load * Inline [
col3,col4
1,2
3,4
5,6
];
```

2. After executing the script, notice that Table Viewer shows one single table, Table1. Even though the column names in the two tables are different, QlikView merged them.

Joins

Joins in QlikView are similar to joins in SQL. Joins between two tables always result in one table. With joins, the columns of the two tables are affected. Joins are explicitly made by using inner join, left join, right join, and outer join.

In QlikView, joins work in the following ways:

- **Inner join**: Only the matching records in the two tables are stored.
- **Left join**: All the records from the first/left table are kept, and only those records from the second table that match a record in the first table are kept.
- **Right join**: All the records from the second/right table are kept, and only those records from the first table that match a record in the second table are kept.
- **Outer join or join**: Records from both the tables will be stored and, where possible, records will be matched.

> Use Joins.qvw to practice different kinds of joins and concatenate options. It is located in your Apps folder.

Join Orders and Order Detail

The Orders and Order Detail tables will be joined because an optimized data model should have only one fact table.

We will use left join between the tables:

1. Use the QlikViewEssentials_Chap3.qvw. Navigate to the **Orders** tab in your script editor.
2. After the load scripts of the Orders table, type left join (Orders).
3. Comment the [Order Detail] table name as this table name will be irrelevant now.

4. Your updated script will appear as follows:

```
1
2   //**********Orders***********
3   Orders:
4   LOAD
5     CustomerID,
6     DueDate,
7     EmployeeID,
8     EmployeeID  As SalesEmployeeID,
9     Freight,
10    OnlineOrderFlag,
11    OnlineOrderFlag  As OnlineOrderFlagCount,
12    OrderDate,
13    Year(OrderDate) As Year,
14    Month(OrderDate) As Month,
15    OrderID,
16    ShipDate,
17    ShipperID,
18    Status,
19    SubTotal,
20    TaxAmt,
21    TerritoryID,
22    TotalDue,
23    ApplyMap('Territory_Map',TerritoryID,'Territory Not Found') As [Order Territory]
24    ;
25  SQL SELECT *
26  FROM OrderHeader;
27
28
29  left join (Orders)                        // This will join Order Detail with Orders. There will be one Orders table in the data model
30  //**********Orders Details***********
31
32  //[Order Detail]:                          // Order Detail name is irrelevant now as it will be combined with the Orders table
33  LOAD *,                                    // This will ensure that all the columns from the previous load are loaded
34  LineTotal  *  (1-Discount) As LineSalesAmount; //Preceding load. Takes LineTotal from the previous load statement
35  LOAD
36    Discount,
37    OrderID,
38    OrderQty              As Quantity,
39    ProductID,
40    UnitPrice,
41    UnitPrice * OrderQty As LineTotal ;
42  SQL SELECT *
43  FROM OrderDetail;
44
```

5. Observe the data model in Table Viewer and you will see the `Orders` and `Order Detail` tables have combined into one table, `Orders`.

Left join SalesPerson

To further optimize your data model, left join `SalesPerson` with the `Orders` table:

1. Navigate to the **Employees** Tab. Go to the `SalesPerson` load script.

2. In the empty space before the load statement, type `left join (Orders)`.

3. This will left join `Orders` and `SalesPerson`. It is good practice to type the table name with left join otherwise it will left join with the previously loaded table script.

4. Save and reload.

5. Observe the `Orders` table in the Table Viewer. `SalesPerson Name` and `SalesPersonTitle` have been added.

Aggregating data

We have combined the `Orders` and `Order Detail` tables; now it is time to find the sales amount for each of these orders by aggregating the data by `OrderID`:

1. Use `QlikViewEssentials_Chap3.qvw`. Navigate to the **Orders** tab in your script editor.

2. Navigate to the empty space after the `Order Detail` load statement.

3. Perform "resident load" from the `Orders` table and aggregate using the `Group By` function. Resident load is used here as the `Orders` table is already loaded in the script and we can reuse the same table using resident load.

4. It will be better to keep `[Order Sales Amt]` in the `Orders` table as it is at the Order level. To achieve this, go to the empty space above the load statement and type `left join(Orders)`.

5. Your script should appear as the following:

```
left Join(Orders)
[Order Aggregate]:
Load
    distinct
        OrderID,
        Sum(LineSalesAmount)  As [Order Sales Amt]
resident Orders
Group By OrderID;
```

Concatenating the new Employees table

As the QlikView development was progressing, Adventure Works Inc. acquired a new company. Now they want to merge the new company's employees into the Adventure Works' `Employees` table.

This can be best achieved by using `Concatenate`, since we know that two tables with the same structure get automatically concatenated. Even if the structure of `NewEmployees` is not the same, we should make it the same so that it concatenates with `Employees`.

The new employee file structure is similar to the Employees table loaded in QlikView.

This new employee file NewEmployees.xlsx is also located in the same location:

1. Navigate to the **Employees** tab in QlikViewEssentials_Chap3.qvw.

2. Go to the empty space after the SalesPerson load script.

3. Click on **Table Files** and browse to NewEmployees.xlsx, which is located under C:\QlikViewEssentials\Data. Make sure to select **Embedded labels** under **Labels** while selecting the file.

4. Remove the directory. Save and reload your script. You will observe just one table, Employees, in the data model and it will have records of both Employees and NewEmployees.

5. The script of the NewEmployees table will appear as the following:

```
//***********New Employees Load ***************************
LOAD EmployeeID,
    [Emp FirstName],
    [Emp MiddleName],
    [Emp LastName],
    JobTitle,
    StartDate,
    EndDate,
    [Emp PhoneNumber],
    [Emp Email Address],
    [Emp Address],
    [Emp City],
    [Emp State],
    [Emp PostalCode],
    [Emp Country]
FROM
[..\Data\NewEmployees.xlsx]
(ooxml, embedded labels, table is Sheet1);
```

Reviewing the final data model

By applying the previous techniques, the data model is being converted into a star schema.

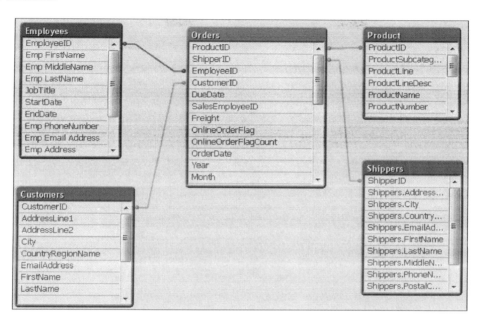

Summary

QlikView always desires a star schema as it is simple to understand and efficient for reporting. In this chapter, we learned different techniques of creating a star schema and converted our previously created data model into a star schema by using mapping loads, joins, and concatenation.

In the next chapter, we will learn about data modeling challenges, which are resolved by using cross tables, link tables, and the master calendar. You will also learn about handling slowly changing dimensions using the `Interval Match` function. Finally we will use QVDs to read and write our data model tables.

4

Data Modeling Challenges

In creating a data model, you will come across challenges in terms of different formats of data, loading multiple fact tables, and performance issues. There are techniques to resolve these challenges.

In this chapter we shall:

- Learn about loading a Crosstable
- Learn about the `Autonumber` function
- Learn about creating a link table to load multiple fact tables
- Learn about variable overview
- Learn about creating a master calendar
- Handle SCD using IntervalMatch
- Store and read data from QVDs (QlikView data files)
- Learn about optimized load
- Discuss best practices for data modeling

Crosstable essentials

In your downloaded folder, look at `EmployeeSalesTarget.xls`. This file is located in `C:\QlikViewEssentials\Data`.

ProductID	EmployeeID	CustomerID	2005	2006	2007	2008
707	276	29522	$100,000.00	$150,000.00	$150,000.00	$100,000.00
707	278	29705	$135,084.17	$209,146.60	$153,340.91	$45,868.91
707	279	29825	$21,262.66	$99,425.74	$131,855.33	$44,393.22
707	281	29489	$46,030.08	$31,052.51	$161,696.18	$83,955.49
707	281	29716	$65,105.68	$230,873.72	$178,004.74	$36,073.44
707	281	29992	$81,562.32	$179,058.09	$119,530.45	$54,923.61
708	276	29522	$100,000.00	$150,000.00	$150,000.00	$100,000.00
708	278	29705	$135,084.17	$209,146.60	$153,340.91	$45,868.91
708	279	29825	$21,262.66	$99,425.74	$131,855.33	$77,193.46
708	281	29489	$46,030.08	$31,052.51	$161,696.18	$148,618.92
708	281	29716	$65,105.68	$301,084.94	$178,004.74	$36,073.44

Some of the properties of this file are as follows:

1. A file of this format is called a Crosstable. A Crosstable is a special format of data in which some of the fields are displayed in rows and some in columns.

2. If this table is loaded in QlikView using a regular load statement, it will load each of the fields separately.

3. The problem with this kind of structure is that the table can grow very large, if each of the fields is stored separately. Performing aggregation on such a table will be difficult. You have do to *Sum(2005) + Sum(2006)* ... to get the total sales.

4. It would be better for QlikView applications to load a table in the following format:

ProductID	CustomerID	EmployeeID	Year	Data
707	29489	281	2005	46030.08
707	29489	281	2006	31052.51
707	29489	281	2007	161696.18
707	29489	281	2008	83955.49
707	29522	276	2005	100000
707	29522	276	2006	150000
707	29522	276	2007	150000
707	29522	276	2008	100000
707	29705	278	2005	135084.17
707	29705	278	2006	209146.6
707	29705	278	2007	153340.91
707	29705	278	2008	45868.91

In this format, the aggregation of data will be much easier.

5. Use the cross table prefix to load a cross table in QlikView.

Loading EmployeeSalesTarget.xlsx

We will load `EmployeeSalesTarget.xlsx` using Crosstable because it is in the Crosstable format:

1. Open `QlikViewEssentials_Chap3.qvw` and save it as `QlikViewEssentials_Chap4_Crosstable.qvw`.

2. Go to the script editor and create a new tab and call it `Crosstable`.

3. Click on **Table Files** and browse to `EmployeeSalesTarget.xlsx`. Check all the default settings and click on **Next**.

4. Click **Next**.

5. Under **File Wizard: Options**, click on **Crosstable** under **Prefixes**.

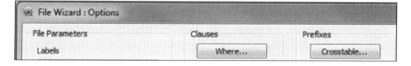

6. Select the **Qualifier Fields, Attribute Field,** and **Data Field**. Qualifier fields are columns on the left. You can specify any number of qualifiers. Attribute and data fields can have any names. The number of qualifier fields are the fields that do not get transformed by Crosstable syntax. Attribute fields are the fields that get transformed. In this case it is `Year`. Attribute Field will transform `Year` under one column. Data Field will contain the data of the attribute field.

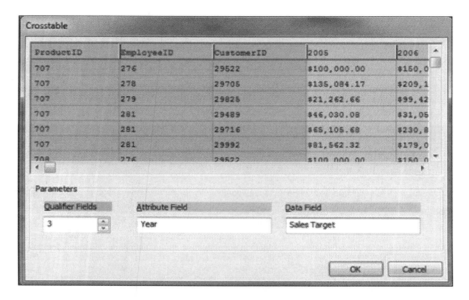

7. Give the name of the table as `SalesTarget`. The load script will appear as follows:

```
SalesTarget:
CrossTable(Year, [Sales Target], 3)
LOAD ProductID,
     EmployeeID,
     CustomerID,
     [2005],
     [2006],
     [2007],
     [2008]
FROM
[..\Data\EmployeeSalesTarget.xls]
(biff, embedded labels, table is SalesTarget$);
```

8. Save and reload. Notice the formation of the synthetic table key and synthetic key due to multiple common fields between the Orders and SalesTarget tables.

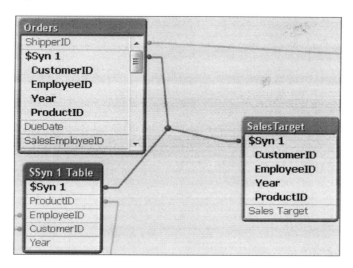

Link table

The previous data model scenario is a typical scenario that occurs due to the presence of multiple fact tables. In this case, Orders and SalesTarget are two fact tables and they share common dimensions. Star schema prefers one single fact table in the schema. This scenario can be resolved with the help of a link table.

A link table is a central table that will contain common fields from the two tables and therefore it creates one table and avoids synthetic keys.

Link table essentials

The following steps are followed in the creation of any link table:

1. Create a composite key in all the concerned fact tables. Use the Autonumber function to make this key unique and numeric. This composite key will act as a key field to connect the link table with fact tables.

2. Load all the common fields from all the fact tables in one table called the link table. Use concatenate for this purpose.

3. Drop these common fields in the original fact table.

Creating a link table

In our data model we have two fact tables: `Orders` and `SalesTarget`. To resolve this, we will create a link table by following the next steps:

1. Use `QlikViewEssentials_Chap4_Crosstable.qvw` and save as `QlikViewEssentials_Chap4_LinkTable.qvw`.

2. Invoke the script editor and create a new tab `Link Table` after the last tab.

3. Identify the common fields in the `Orders` and `SalesTarget` tables. These common fields are `Year`, `CustomerID`, `EmployeeID`, and `ProductID`.

4. Create a new table `EmpSalesTarget`. This table will be created from the `SalesTarget` table. The `SalesTarget` table was created when we loaded the Crosstable in the previous section. We will load all the fields from the `SalesTarget` table using resident load. The `SalesTarget` table contains the common fields. We will create a composite key using the common fields and name it `KeyField`. Use the `Autonumber` function to create unique integer values for `%KeyField`:

```
Autonumber(Year & '|' & CustomerID & '|' & EmployeeID & '|' & ProductID) As %KeyField
```

 `Autonumber` is a very important function in QlikView. It is used to convert strings into unique numbers. In the absence of the `Autonumber` function, the previous composite field will be a string field and will not be better suited for joining the two tables. It will also take more memory as compared to a numeric field.

5. Drop the `SalesTarget` table as this table is no longer needed. The contents of this table are loaded into the `EmpSalesTarget` table. Your script will look as follows:

```
EmpSalesTarget:
Load
    *,    //Load all the fields from SalesTarget

    Autonumber(Year & '|' & CustomerID & '|' & EmployeeID & '|' & ProductID) As %KeyField

Resident SalesTarget;

Drop Table SalesTarget; //Drop SalesTarget as it is not required now.
```

6. Create another table, `Facts`. This table is created to have a clean table that contains the fields from `Orders`, `OrderDetails`, and `Order Aggregate` tables. Resident load will be used to achieve this because the `Orders` table is already present in the memory. Create a composite key in the `Orders` table, similar to the `EmpSalesTarget` table. Drop the table `Orders` as it is no longer needed.

```
Facts:
Load
    *, //Load all the fields from Orders
    Autonumber(Year & '|' & CustomerID & '|' & EmployeeID & '|' & ProductID) As %KeyField
    Resident Orders;

Drop Table Orders; //Drop Orders as it is not required now.
```

7. In the next two steps, create a new table and name it `LinkTable`, which will hold common fields from both the previous tables. Make sure that you load distinct fields only in order to avoid duplicates.

8. Perform resident load from the `Facts` table and store the distinct combinations in the link table. Create a duplicate `%KeyField` and name it `%TempKeyField`. This field will be used while loading data from `EmpSalesTarget`.

```
LinkTable:
Load
    Distinct
    %KeyField,
    %KeyField As %TempKeyField,
    Year,
    CustomerID,
    EmployeeID,
    ProductID
Resident Facts;
```

9. Concatenate distinct common fields from the `EmpSalesTarget` table. Use `%TempKeyField` to make sure that `%KeyField` from the `EmpSalesTarget` table does not exist in the fields from `Facts`. After loading this statement, drop `%TempKeyField` as it was required only for comparison.

```
Concatenate(LinkTable)
Load
    Distinct
    %KeyField,
    Year,
    CustomerID,
    EmployeeID,
    ProductID
Resident EmpSalesTarget
where Not Exists(%TempKeyField,%KeyField);

Drop Field %TempKeyField from LinkTable;
```

10. Once the link table is created and loaded, drop the fields that are no longer required. Drop the common fields from `Facts` and `EmpSalesTarget` as these fields are now stored in the link table.

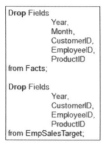

```
Drop Fields
        Year,
        Month,
        CustomerID,
        EmployeeID,
        ProductID
from Facts;

Drop Fields
        Year,
        CustomerID,
        EmployeeID,
        ProductID
from EmpSalesTarget;
```

11. Your overall link table script will appear as follows:

```
 2  EmpSalesTarget:
 3  Load
 4      *,      //Load all the fields from SalesTarget
 5
 6      Autonumber(Year & ┬ & CustomerID & ┬ & EmployeeID & ┬ & ProductID) As %KeyField
 7
 8  Resident SalesTarget;
 9
10  Drop Table SalesTarget; //Drop SalesTarget as it is not required now.
11
12  Facts:
13  Load
14      *,      //Load all the fields from Orders
15      Autonumber(Year & ┬ & CustomerID & ┬ & EmployeeID & ┬ & ProductID) As %KeyField
16      Resident Orders;
17
18  Drop Table Orders; //Drop Orders as it is not required now
19
20  LinkTable:
21  Load
22      Distinct
23      %KeyField,
24      %KeyField As %TempKeyField,
25      Year,
26      CustomerID,
27      EmployeeID,
28      ProductID
29  Resident Facts;
30
31  Concatenate(LinkTable)
32  Load
33      Distinct
34      %KeyField,
35      Year,
36      CustomerID,
37      EmployeeID,
38      ProductID
39  Resident EmpSalesTarget
40  where Not Exists(%TempKeyField,%KeyField);
41
42  Drop Field %TempKeyField from LinkTable;
43
44  Drop Fields
45          Year,
46          Month,
47          CustomerID,
48          EmployeeID,
49          ProductID
50  from Facts;
51
52  Drop Fields
53          Year,
54          CustomerID,
55          EmployeeID,
56          ProductID
57  from EmpSalesTarget;
58
```

A link table should be used with caution. As the size of the link table grows, performance degrades.

Concatenating two fact tables is also an efficient way to merge two fact tables.

 Link tables and concatenate are both ways to merge the fact tables. Use concatenate when granularity of the tables and dimensions they connect to are the same. Use link tables when granularity of the tables and connected dimensions are different.

After creating a link table, the resulting data model will appear as follows:

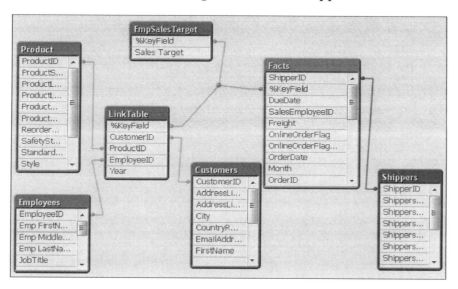

Variables in QlikView

Variables are used to store static values or expressions. Variables make it easy to reuse expressions.

In QlikView, variables can be declared in the script or by invoking Variable Overview by pressing *Ctrl + Alt +V*. It can also be declared by navigating to **Settings** from menu and clicking on **Variable Overview**. Variables declared in the script can be seen in Variable Overview too.

In the script, variables are declared using `Set` and `Let` statements.

The `Set` statement assign literal strings to the variable, and the `Let` statement first evaluates the string and then assigns it to a variable:

```
Set vVariable1 =  1 +  3;  //Value of vVariable1 is 1  + 3
Let vVariable2 =  1 + 3;  //Value of vVariable2 is 4
```

It is important to discuss "dollar sign expansion" while discussing variables. Dollar sign expansions are definitions of text replacement. $(text) syntax expands the text that is between the $ sign and the parenthesis, and then it is evaluated. So an expression such as $(=1+3) will evaluate as 4 instead of 1 + 3.

Using variables to set the file path

Variables can also be used in setting the path of a file, for example, while loading an xlsx file from the location `[..\Data\Employees.xlsx]`, you can use a variable and set this path for all the Excel files, for example:

```
Set vExcelpath =..\Data\;
```

And use the variable to load the xlsx file from this location:

```
$(vExcelpath)Employees.xlsx
```

Using variables to set the path of a file is useful for ease of maintenance. In case the path of the file changes, you just need to change the value of the variable.

Variable definitions can be checked and defined by going into Variable Overview. Use *Ctrl + Alt + V* to invoke Variable Overview.

Master calendar

As a best practice, it is always better to keep time-related fields in a separate table outside of the fact table. This is particularly helpful when you want to see all the dates, and not just the dates when specific events occurred. In our case, we should be able to see all the dates, and not just the dates when an order was made, because in real-life scenarios there may be days or months in which no order was made. It is also important to remember that QlikView stores dates as numbers:

1. Use the same QVW file `QlikViewEssentials_Chap4_LinkTable.qvw`.
2. Invoke the script editor. Navigate to the **Orders** Tab. Go to the load script of `Orders` and comment the `Month` field by using `//`. We will be creating this field in the master calendar.

3. Create a new tab after the **LinkTable** tab and name it `Master Calendar`.

4. Get min and max dates. Create a new table `GetDateRange` and load min and max dates from the `Facts` table. QlikView stores dates as numbers. You can subtract the dates by converting numbers to dates, and vice versa. This will create the lower range and upper range of the calendar.

```
GetDateRange: // Getting Min and Max dates from Facts
LOAD
    Min(OrderDate) As MinDate,
    Max(OrderDate) As MaxDate
Resident Facts;
```

5. Store min and max dates in variables. Create two variables to store the min and max dates from the table `GetDateRange`. Notice the use of `Peek`:

```
// Peek is used to get the MinDate and MaxDate from the first row
Let vMinDate = Peek('MinDate', 0 ,'GetDateRange');
Let vMaxDate = Peek('MaxDate', 0 ,'GetDateRange');
```

A word about Peek:

The syntax for `Peek` is as follows:

```
Peek (fieldname [ , row [ , tablename ] ] )
```

This function returns the contents of the `fieldname` in the record specified by `row` in the table `tablename`. The field name and table name should be in quotes.

Note that row number starts with 0. So the first row is 0, the second row is 1, and so on. If no number is specified, -1 is assumed, which denotes the last row.

In the previous statement, 0 is specified with `Peek` because the `GetDateRange` table has only one row.

6. Create `TempCalendar` to store list of dates. Create a table `TempCalendar` by using the recently created variables. Here, two new functions are used: `RowNo` and `Autogenerate`:

   ° `RowNo` returns an integer for the position of the current row in the table. It has values such as 1, 2, 3, and so on.

○ `Autogenerate` is used to automatically generate data by QlikView. Its parameter is size, which is an integer for the number of rows to be generated.

```
TempCalendar:
Load
    date($(vMinDate) + RowNo() -1) as TempDate  // First RownNo is 1
AutoGenerate $(vMaxDate) - $(vMinDate) + 1;     // This will generate number of rows between MaxDate and Mindate +1
```

In this statement, RowNo 1 is used because we want to include the `MinDate` in the list of dates. `AutoGenerate` uses `AutoGenerate $(vMaxDate) - $(vMinDate) + 1;` because we want to include the maximum date in the list of dates.

7. Finally, create the `MasterCalendar` table by performing a resident load from the `TempCalendar` table. Create all the required date fields such as `Day`, `Week`, `Month`, `Year`, and `Quarter`. Make sure to rename `TempDate` to `OrderDate` so that it can link with the `Facts` table. Drop the `GetDateRange` and `TempCalendar` tables as they are not required now.

The `MasterCalendar` script will look like the following:

```
 1
 2  GetDateRange: // Getting Min and Max dates from Facts
 3  LOAD
 4      Min(OrderDate) As MinDate,
 5      Max(OrderDate) As MaxDate
 6  Resident Facts;
 7
 8  Let vMinDate = Peek('MinDate', 0 ,'GetDateRange');  // Peek is used to get the MinDate from the first row
 9  Let vMaxDate = Peek('MaxDate', 0 ,'GetDateRange');//Peek is used to get the MinDate from the first row
10
11  TempCalendar:
12  Load
13      date($(vMinDate) + RowNo() -1) as TempDate  // First RownNo is 1
14  AutoGenerate $(vMaxDate) - $(vMinDate) + 1;       // This will generate number of rows between MaxDate and Mindate +1
15
16
17  MasterCalendar:
18  LOAD
19      TempDate            As  OrderDate,  //Rename to OrderDate to link with Facts table
20      Day(TempDate)       As  Day,
21      Year(TempDate)      As  CalendarYear,
22      Month(TempDate)     As  Month,
23      Week(TempDate)      As  Week,
24      'Q' & Ceil(month(TempDate)/3) As Quarter,
25      Date(MonthStart(TempDate), 'MMM-YYYY') As  MonthYear
26
27      Resident TempCalendar
28      Order by TempDate asc;
29
30      Drop table GetDateRange; //This table is no longer needed
31      Drop Table TempCalendar; //This table is no longer needed
```

8. Review the `MasterCalendar` table in the Table Viewer.

The IntervalMatch function

The `IntervalMatch` function is used to match a single value in a table to an interval or range of values in another table. This scenario occurs in real time when you are trying to match a date in one table, which falls between two dates in another table. Another example will be matching the number of shifts falling in a time period of, say, eight hours.

The `IntervalMatch` function is also useful in handling slowly changing dimensions (SCD), specifically Type 2.

Slowly changing dimension Type 2 is used to track the historical information of the data. For example, see the following employee records:

EmployeeID	FirstName	MiddleName	LastName	JobTitle	StartDate	EndDate
275	Michael	G	Blythe	Sales Representative	2/12/2003	12/1/2007
275	Michael	G	Blythe	Sales Manager	1/2/2007	9/99/9999
278	Garrett	R	Vargas	Sales Manager	1/24/2003	12/31/2005
278	Garrett	R	Vargas	Sales Representative	1/1/2006	9/99/9999

Employees with IDs 275 and 278 have held two positions respectively. This table is an SCD Type 2 because it stores the information for both the positions using a start date and an end date. The end date of 9/99/9999 represents that the position is still open and not end-dated.

The data modeling challenge is to find out which position or job titles they held during a specific time period.

In our Adventure Works data model, we want to know when a certain order was made, and which job titles were held by these employees. The `Orders` table contains `OrderDate`, `StartDate`, and `EndDate` in the `Employees` table.

In SQL, you can link the two tables using a `Between` clause. In QlikView, this is achieved by using IntervalMatch's extended syntax:

1. Use `QlikViewEssentials_Chap4_LinkTable.qvw` and save it as `QlikViewEssentials_Chap4_IntervalMatch.qvw`.

2. We will use `Employees.xlsx` as our slowly changing dimensions. Notice the previous records in the `Employees.xlsx` for employee ID 275 and 278. They have changed job titles over time. Using `IntervalMatch`, we will find out which job titles were held by these employees when a specific order was made.

3. Navigate to the **Dimensions** tab and go to the load script of `Employees`. Create a dummy field for `SalesEmployeeID` using the `EmployeeID` field. Go to the bottom of the sheet and make a similar change in the load script for `NewEmployees` too.

   ```
   EmployeeID As SalesEmployeeID,
   ```

4. Use Preceding Load to create a composite key using `StartDate`, `EndDate`, and `SalesEmployeeID`. To create a Preceding Load, go to the empty space above the Employees' `Load` and type the following statement. Go to the bottom of the sheet and make a similar change in the load script for `NewEmployees` too.

   ```
   LOAD
       *,        //This will load all the fields from the previous load
       StartDate &'|'& EndDate &'|'& SalesEmployeeID  As  IntervalComposite;
   ```

5. Create a new tab and name it `IntervalMatch`. Make sure that this tab is the last tab in your script editor.

6. Create a table `IntervalMatch`. Here we will use the `IntervalMatch` function's extended syntax:

   ```
   intervalmatch (matchfield,keyfield1 [ , keyfield2, ... keyfield5 ]
   )
    (loadstatement | selectstatement )
   ```

7. The extended `IntervalMatch` is used to create a table matching a single numeric value to numeric intervals of range, while matching the values of one or several keys.

8. In this example, `matchfield` is `OrderDate` and `SalesEmployeeID` is the `Keyfield`.

9. This means that `OrderDate` will be matched against the `StartDate` and `EndDate` of an employee to get the `JobTitle` of the employee using `SalesEmployeeID` as the key field.

10. The `IntervalMatch` syntax will appear as follows:

    ```
    IntervalMatch:
    IntervalMatch(OrderDate,SalesEmployeeID)   //IntervalMatch extended syntax
    Load
        StartDate,
        EndDate,
        SalesEmployeeID
    Resident Employees;
    ```

11. Resident load from the `IntervalMatch` table and left join with `Facts` to avoid a synthetic key. Drop the table `IntervalMatch` as it is not required now. Drop the field `SalesEmployeeID` from the `Facts` and `Employees` table. Drop `EmployeeID` from the `Employees` table. These fields are not required now.

12. The script for the **IntervalMatch** tab will appear like the one shown as follows. Save and reload.

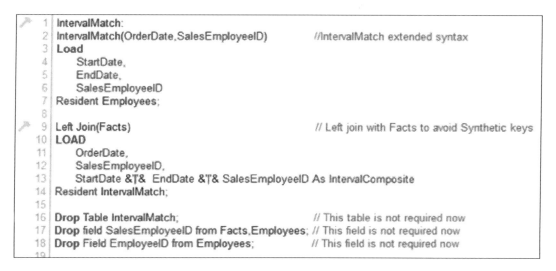

```
1  IntervalMatch:
2  IntervalMatch(OrderDate,SalesEmployeeID)        //IntervalMatch extended syntax
3  Load
4      StartDate,
5      EndDate,
6      SalesEmployeeID
7  Resident Employees;
8
9  Left Join(Facts)                                 // Left join with Facts to avoid Synthetic keys
10 LOAD
11     OrderDate,
12     SalesEmployeeID,
13     StartDate &'|'& EndDate &'|'& SalesEmployeeID As IntervalComposite
14 Resident IntervalMatch;
15
16 Drop Table IntervalMatch;                        // This table is not required now
17 Drop field SalesEmployeeID from Facts,Employees; // This field is not required now
18 Drop Field EmployeeID from Employees;            // This field is not required now
19
```

13. Check your data model in Table Viewer. Now the `Facts` and `Employees` tables will link based on the `IntervalComposite` field.

14. To test your application, close the script editor. Go to the empty space in your sheet and create the following list boxes. You can see that `OrderDate` 7/1/2005 falls between `StartDate` and `EndDate` of 2/12/20013 and 12/1/2007 respectively. During that time, Michael Blythe's job title was Sales Representative.

OrderDate	EmployeeID	SalesPerson Name	JobTitle	StartDate	EndDate
7/1/2005	275	Michael Blythe	Sales Representative	2/12/2003	12/1/2007
8/1/2005	274	David Campbell	Accountant	7/31/2000	9/99/9999
9/1/2005	276	Garrett Vargas	Accounts Manager	2/26/2001	8/15/2003
10/1/2005	277	Jillian Carson	Accounts Payable Spec	12/12/2001	6/30/2004
11/1/2005	278	José Saraiva	Accounts Receivable S	1/5/2002	8/30/2005
12/1/2005	279	Linda Mitchell	Application Specialist	1/11/2002	10/1/2005
1/1/2006	280	Pamela Ansman-Wolfe	Assistant to the Chief F	1/20/2002	12/31/2005
2/1/2006	281	Shu Ito	Benefits Specialist	1/26/2002	8/15/2006
3/1/2006	282	Tsvi Reiter	Buyer	2/6/2002	1/1/2007
4/1/2006	283	Amy Alberts	Chief Executive Officer	2/7/2002	
5/1/2006	284			2/24/2002	
	285				
	286				

QlikView Data Files (QVD)

A QVD file is a very important feature in QlikView. It is a file containing a table of data exported from QlikView:

- QVD is a native QlikView format, meaning it can be read/write only from QlikView.

- Reading data from a QVD file is typically 10-100 times faster than reading from other data sources. It reduces the load on the database as QVDs can be loaded once and used multiple times without connecting to the database.

- QVD files can be shared easily among different applications.

- QVD files can combine data from multiple QlikView documents.

- An incremental load is implemented using QVD files.

- A QVD file consists of:
    - A well-formed XML header
    - Symbol tables in a byte stuffed format
    - Actual tables of data in a bit stuffed format

- QVD is created by using a STORE command.

Creating QVD files for our data model

We will store all the tables in the QVD files so that data read and write is faster:

1. Open QlikViewEssentials_Chap4_IntervalMatch.qvw and save as QlikViewEssentials_Chap4_QVDCreator.qvw.

2. Go to the **Main** tab and set the variable for the QVD path, the path where the QVD will be stored. You already have a QVD folder in your downloaded folder. You can either create a relative path or use the absolute path C:\ QlikViewEssentials\Data\Qvds.

3. Create a variable vQVDpath as follows:

    ```
    SET vQVDpath = ..\Data\Qvds;
    ```

4. Skip the **Mapping** tab as these tables are temporary tables, and drop after script execution. Skip the **Orders** tab as the Orders table gets dropped in the **LinkTable** tab.

5. Navigate to the **Dimensions** tab. Go to the empty space below the Customers' `Load` statement and use the `STORE` command to store this table into QVD. Make sure you use the correct table name next to `STORE`. Type the following statement:

```
STORE Customers into $(vQVDpath)Customers.qvd;
```

6. You can always use a hard absolute path if you don't want to use the variable. Save and reload the script.

7. Go to your Windows Explorer and notice that `Customers.qvd` is created in the path specified.

8. Follow similar steps to store all the other tables in the QVDs.

9. Go to the empty space below the `Load` script of the `Product` table and type:

```
STORE Product into $(vQVDpath)Product.qvd;
```

   Save and reload the script.

10. Go to the empty space below the `Load` script of `Shippers` and use:

```
STORE Shippers into $(vQVDpath)Shippers.qvd;
```

   Save and reload the script.

11. Skip the **Employees** tab as we do a lot of transformation to this table in the **IntervalMatch** tab.

12. Skip the **CrossTable** tab as this table is later dropped in the **LinkTable** tab.

13. Navigate to the **LinkTable** tab. Go to the empty space all the way at the bottom, after all the script statements. We want to store the tables in QVD after all the transformation is done:

```
STORE LinkTable into $(vQVDpath)LinkTable.qvd;
STORE EmpSalesTarget into $(vQVDpath)EmpSalesTarget.qvd;
```

   Save and reload the script.

14. Navigate to the **MasterCalendar** tab. Go all the way down to the empty space after all the script space and type:

```
STORE MasterCalendar into $(vQVDpath)MasterCalendar.qvd;
```

   Save and reload the script.

15. Navigate to the **IntervalMatch** tab and go to the empty space all the way at the bottom and type:

```
STORE Employees into $(vQVDpath)Employees.qvd;
STORE Facts into $(vQVDpath)Facts.qvd;
```

Save and reload the script.

16. Go your Windows Explorer and check whether all the QVDs have been created in the path specified. Count the number of QVDs. It should be the same as the number of tables in the data model.

Customers.qvd

Employees.qvd

EmpSalesTarget.qvd

Facts.qvd

LinkTable.qvd

MasterCalendar.qvd

Product.qvd

Shippers.qvd

Optimized load – reading QVD

In the previous section, we have stored data into QVDs. Now it is time to read or load from a QVD. QVDs can be read as a regular load or as an optimized load.

An optimized load is a super-fast load that occurs if no transformations occur or certain conditions are applied. An optimized load is indicated by the message in the script progress window.

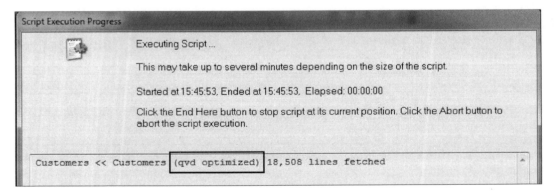

The following conditions apply to an optimized load:

1. Renaming a field is allowed.

2. Data transformation is not allowed.

3. You cannot add new fields.

4. "where exists" on a single field is allowed. However, `Where Exists(EmpID,SalesID)` is not allowed.

5. "where exists" is not allowed to rename the fields.

Reading QVD files

Reading data from QVD is faster than reading from a database. Once data is stored in the QVD, follow the next steps to read from the QVDs:

1. If not open already, open the QlikView desktop. Create a new QVD by using **File | New**. Save this file as `QlikViewEssentials_DataModel.qvw`.

2. Invoke the script editor by pressing *Ctrl + E* or by clicking on the script editor icon.

3. Create a new tab and call it **Dimensions**.

4. Click on **Table Files** as QVD is also loaded like any other file. Browse to your QVD folder where all the QVDs are loaded. Select `Customers.qvd`.

5. Click on **Finish**.

6. Remove the directory and name this table as `Customers`. Save and reload the script.

7. The QVD load script looks like the one shown as follows:

```
Products:
LOAD ProductID,
    ProductSubcategoryID,
    ProductLine,
    ProductLineDesc,
    ProductName,
    ProductNumber,
    ReorderPoint,
    SafetyStockLevel,
    StandardCost,
    Style,
    ListPrice,
    [SubCategory Desc],
    [Category Desc]
FROM
[..\Data\Qvds\Product.qvd]
(qvd);
```

8. Load all the QVDs for the **Dimensions** tab in a similar fashion. These QVDs will be for `Products`, `Employees`, `EmpSalesTarget`, and `Shippers`.

9. Create a new tab and name it `Facts`. Load `Facts.qvd` in this tab.

10. Create a new tab for the `LinkTable` and load `LinkTable.qvd` in this tab.

11. Create a new tab for `MasterCalendar` and load `MasterCalendar.qvd` in this tab.

12. Save and reload the script. All the tables are loaded with optimized load.

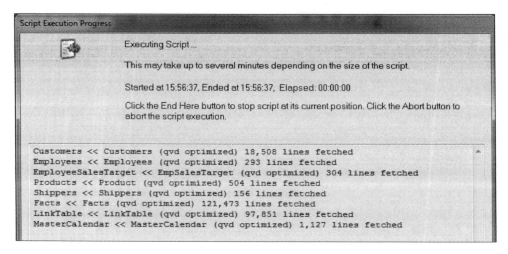

13. Review your data model in the Table Viewer.

Best practices of data modeling

In the previous chapters, we learned how to create a data model in QlikView. While creating a data model, it is always recommended to follow the best practices so that the data model is reusable and performs better.

The following best practices of data modeling will ensure a robust data model. It will also recap what we learned so far:

- **Associations**: In QlikView, associations are created based on common field names between the two tables. Associations should be created based on the business context between the tables. To create or break associations, table columns can be renamed. Wrong associations will result in wrong outputs.

- Organize your script. Data load scripts should be organized by creating tabs in the script editor. Related subject matter should be on the same tab.

- The first tab of the script should contain author and versioning information.

- Author information and versioning is important for change control purposes.

- Comment your code for better understanding. A well-commented code helps in understanding the code. It also helps in future enhancements.

- Use Include files. All the information that can be shared across applications should be kept in files, which can be included in the QlikView document.

- Use variables for ease of maintenance and portability.

- Load only the required fields and tables. Since every field is loaded in the memory, only the tables and fields required for creating visualizations should be loaded for better performance.

- Provide business names to the table columns. Source data field names may be database-specific and will be difficult to provide information to the users. Alias your field names to business-specific names.

- QVDs should be used wherever possible. Reading data from QVDs is much faster than reading from the database tables. QVDs also provide a good way of sharing information between the organizational units.

- Use multi-level QVD architecture to create a robust data model. Data models should be created by designing multi-level QVD architecture.

    ◦ The first layer should be an extract layer in which raw data from the tables is extracted and loaded in the QVDs.

    ◦ The second layer should be a transformation layer. All data transformation should be done in this layer and should be stored in QVDs.

    ◦ The third layer should be a presentation layer. For better performance, optimized load from the QVDs should be performed in this layer.

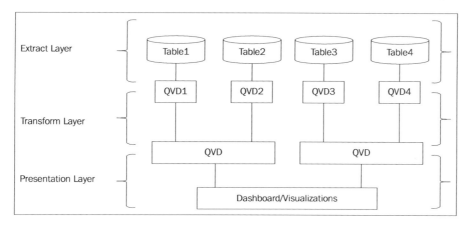

- Remove synthetic keys. When multiple tables are loaded, there may be occurrences of multiple common columns between multiple tables. This will create complex keys or synthetic keys. Synthetic keys are resource heavy and will slow down the application. It may also make the data model complex and hard to understand. In extreme cases, it may result in incorrect data. Synthetic keys should be eliminated from the data model.

- Remove circular references. Circular references or loops occur in the data model when there is more than one path to a table. Such occurrences should be avoided because it may lead to ambiguous representation of data.

- Have a simple data model design. QlikView recommends that the data model design should be simple. The number of tables and joins should be reduced and the data model should be clean. This can be achieved by the use of mapping load and apply map functionality in QlikView.

- Create a master calendar. A master calendar should be created to maintain all the time dimension values. This table helps if the fact table does not have continuous dates.

Summary

In this chapter, we learned about resolving data modeling challenges by loading a Crosstable and a link table. We also learned about the importance and creation of a master calendar.

Slowly changing dimensions are also handled using the `IntervalMatch` function.

Once done with all the data transformations, we loaded tables in QVDs, as reading data from QVDs is faster than reading from a database. We learned about optimized load to improve data load performance. This finished the scripting and data modeling in QlikView. This chapter also provided the best practices of data modeling that should be followed in order to create a better performing data model.

In upcoming chapters, we will learn about creating visualizations in QlikView using the data model we created so far. In the next chapter, we will learn about data visualization best practices and will create different charts and tables.

5

Creating Dashboards

Previous chapters dealt with creating data models in QlikView. They laid the foundation for creating interactive visualizations or dashboards. A dashboard is a pictorial representation of data using charts and tables.

In this chapter, we shall:

- Learn the best practices of visualization
- Learn about binary load
- Learn about different visualization objects in QlikView
- Learn how to create different kinds of charts
- Learn about a few important functions

Dashboarding essentials

Dashboard or visualization applications are a pictorial representation of data.

- They provide executives and analysts with insight into an organization's **key performance indicators** (**KPIs**) to make business decisions. They give users a snapshot of the KPIs and the ability to see the details of the data.

- Dashboards involve creating various visualization objects and placing them on screen in a way that provides users with ease of both understanding and accessing the information.

- As dashboard helps in understanding data, care should be given to engage users with the data. Overuse of colors should be avoided. Attempts should be made to avoid any object that does not represent data.

- Edward Tufte, the author of *The Visual Display of Quantitative Information, Graphics Press USA,* provides principles for visualizing large quantities of data. His book states that data graphics should draw the viewer's attention to the sense and substance of data, not to something else. Non-data pixels should be minimized. Non-data pixels are represented by 3D objects, borders, grid lines, shadows, and glossy colors. Such objects should have a minimal presence on the dashboard.

- Visualizations designed in QlikView are referred to as a dashboard, document, or application. They display data in multiple sheets or tabs and show data regarding one business area. In QlikView, .qvw is referred to as a document.

- For a better user experience, the look and feel of the entire application and all the other applications in the organization should be the same. Create a template with layout standards and create standards for object size, color, font size, and so on. Use this template to create all the dashboards for an organization.

- The dashboard should always be created for the target user group screen resolution. The resolution should be set according to the most commonly used resolution on a user's laptop.

- Document properties from the **File** menu can be used to get details on a document. Documents contain sheets and sheets contain objects.

- As a general practice, the following screen layout is practiced when creating a visualization application in QlikView:

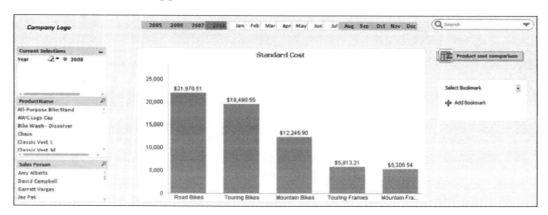

Note the following observations in the preceding screen layout:

- ° Time-related list boxes are situated in the top center
- ° Company logo, current selection box, and list boxes to filter the data are positioned on the left
- ° Charts are in the middle, and any other objects on the right side

Getting started

Let's start by understanding different concepts in building a dashboard application using QlikView.

Associative experience

In QlikView, data is always associated. As we learned in previous chapters, two tables can be associated based on common field names. All the data is present, all the time. Users can click on any list box; the selected data element in the list box turns *green*, the associated data elements in the other list boxes appear in *white*, and the data not associated appears in *gray*.

This can be best depicted in the following screenshot. This is taken from the `QlikView Movies Database.qvw` file located in the QlikView installation folder under `\Program Files\QlikView\Examples\Documents`.

Green shows the selection made in a list box. Associated data elements appear in *white* and data elements not associated appear in *gray*. In this example, the user clicks on **Apple**, so **Apple** appears in *green*. Apple can be *green* or *red*, so these appear in *white*. Apple cannot be *yellow*, and thus appears in *gray*.

To clear selections, users can click on the **Clear** button on the toolbar and make other selections.

Binary load

Binary load can be used to hide the complexity of scripting from the QlikView designer. Binary statement or binary load is used to load data from another QlikView document. It does not load layout information or variables. Only one binary statement is allowed in the script and it should be the first statement of a script:

1. Open the QlikView desktop. Create a new file and save this file as `QlikViewEssentials_Presentation.qvw`.

2. Invoke script editor by pressing *Ctrl + E*. On the **Main** tab, go to the empty space all the way up before the default variable declarations.

3. From the bottom **Data from the files** section, click on the **QlikView File** button which appears like this: QlikView File... .

4. Browse to `QlikViewEssentials_datamodel.qvw`, which you created in the previous chapter, and click on **OK**.

5. Save and reload your script. Use table viewer to view your data model. All the tables are created and the data is being loaded.

6. Your binary load script will appear like the following:

```
Binary qlikviewessentials_datamodel.qvw; // Use Binary to load scripts from another qvw

SET ThousandSep=',';
SET DecimalSep='.';
SET MoneyThousandSep=',';
SET MoneyDecimalSep='.';
SET MoneyFormat='$#,##0.00;($#,##0.00)';
SET TimeFormat='h:mm:ss TT';
SET DateFormat='M/D/YYYY';
SET TimestampFormat='M/D/YYYY h:mm:ss[.fff] TT';
SET MonthNames='Jan;Feb;Mar;Apr;May;Jun;Jul;Aug;Sep;Oct;Nov;Dec';
SET DayNames='Mon;Tue;Wed;Thu;Fri;Sat;Sun';
```

Exploring menu items

You have explored different options in the menu in the previous chapters. Here we will explore some important options with respect to creating visualizations. We will also make changes as required:

1. Use `QlikViewEssentials_Presentation.qvw`.

2. From the menu, click on **View**. View can be used to add or remove **Toolbars**. Use resize to select the screen resolution.

3. For this application, select a resolution of **1280 * 1024** from the **Resize Window** option.

4. **Design Grid** is used for sizing and placing objects on the sheet. **Turn on/ off WebView** uses the internal web browser in QlikView to display the document in AJAX mode.

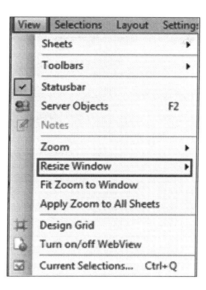

5. From the menu, click on **Layout**. This option is used to add sheets to the layout. The **New Sheet Object** option is used to add sheet objects such as list boxes, textboxes, charts, and so on.

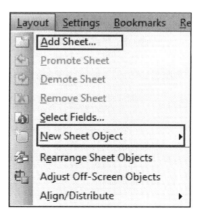

6. From the **File** menu, click on **Settings**. This option is used to configure user preferences and document properties. Some of these configurations you have done in *Chapter 2, Extract, Transform, and Load,* under the *Configuring settings* section. **Variable Overview** is used to create and define variables. **Expression Overview** shows all the expressions in the document. You can edit/find or replace any single or multiple expressions.

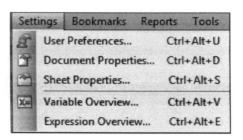

7. **Bookmarks** and **Reports** menu items are used for creating bookmarks and reports.

Sheet objects

Before embarking on our journey of designing visualizations, let's get familiar with different sheet objects. A QlikView document can have one or more sheets. These sheets will contain many objects. They are called objects or sheet objects because they reside on a sheet. In QlikView, every component has an ID. Sheets have a sheet ID and all other components have object IDs. Throughout the application, sheets and objects can be referred by these IDs. You can modify the properties of all the objects according to your requirements.

Right-click on an empty space on a sheet. Hover over **New Sheet Object** to get the list of sheet objects available to you. From the following screenshot, you can also see that you can copy and paste sheets. You can copy and paste sheet objects too.

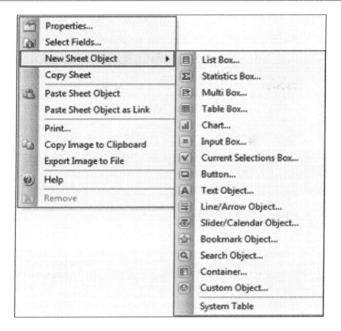

The list of sheet objects available to you are:

- **List Box** is used to filter the data.

- **Statistics Box** is a compact way to display a numeric field with default functions such as sum, min, max, average.

- **Multi Box**, as opposed to **List Box**, can display multiple fields in one object.

- **Table Box** is used to display fields from one or more tables. **Table Box** does not have dimensions or expressions.

- **Chart** is a graphical representation of data. There are different types of chart in QlikView: Bar, Line, Combo, Radar, Scatter, Grid, Pie, Funnel, Block, and Gauge charts. Pivot table and straight table also come under charts.

- **Input Box** is used for entering data in QlikView variables and displaying their values.

- **Current Selections Box** displays selected fields on the application. It lists the selections by field name and field value.

- **Button** is used to perform commands or actions.

- **Text Object** is used for adding information to the document, such as labels, and so on. Text objects can also be used for calculations.

- **Line/Arrow Object** is used to add lines or arrows in the layout.

- **Slider/Calendar Object** provides an alternative means for selecting field values. They can also be used for entering values in the QlikView variable.

- **Bookmark Object** is used for displaying bookmarks for selections.

- **Search Object** is used for searching for information anywhere in the document. All the fields or lists of fields can be searched using a search object.

- **Container** can contain all other sheet objects. The objects are grouped together and have common settings for font, layout, and caption.

- **Custom Object** is specifically intended to carry custom-defined OCX replacement controls.

- **System Table** is a special type of pivot table, showing the data structure of the document. The system table uses system fields. Fields are prefixed with $.

Creating a multi-tab application

When a new QVW is created, a sheet with the title Main is created by default. This is the first sheet and it can be used to give details about the dashboard. We will create this tab to give the details about our dashboard application:

1. Right-click on the empty space on the sheet and go to **Properties....** Change the **Title** of the sheet from Main to About and click on **OK**.

2. Right-click on the empty space on the sheet and hover over **New Sheet Object** and select **Text Object**.

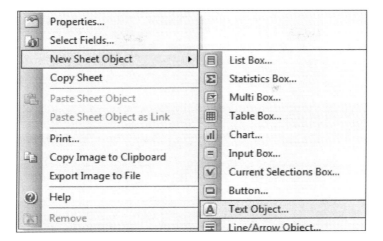

3. On the **General** tab, under **Text**, type the following:

   "Adventure Works Cycles, is a large, multinational manufacturing company. The company manufactures and sells metal and composite bicycles.

   This dashboard is built to provide data insights into their customers, sales and products."

4. Under **Layout**, change **Horizontal Alignment** to **Left** and **Vertical Alignment** to **Top**.

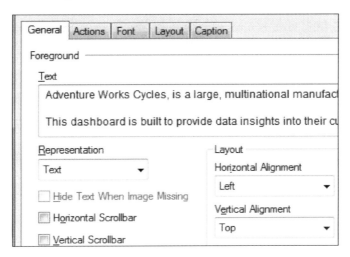

5. Click on the **Font** tab, change the font to **Calibri** and font size to **16**.

6. Click on **Ok**. To see the whole text, hover over the textbox edges until you see the drag icon. Drag the textbox corners to expand the textbox.

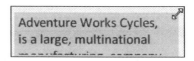

7. Right-click on the textbox to go to **Properties**. On the **General** tab, change **Transparency** to **100%**.

8. A text object can also contain an image. Create another text object. On the **General** tab, under **Background**, click on **Image**. Browse to `logo.png` in your image folder and click **Ok**.

9. Save your application. Your `About` sheet should appear like the one shown in the following screenshot:

> *AWC Inc.*
>
> Adventure Works Cycles, is a large, multinational manufacturing company. The company manufactures and sells metal and composite bicycles.
>
> This dashboard is built to provide data insights into their customers, sales and products.

The dashboard sheet

We will create a new sheet called `Dashboard`. This sheet will display charts and tables, which users will use for their analysis. The business requirement of this sheet is that the business executives will be able to get a snapshot of the company with respect to sales and orders:

1. From the `Layout` menu, click on **Add Sheet...** or use the **Add Sheet** button.

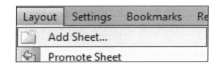

2. From the **General** tab, change the **Title** of the sheet to `Dashboard` by going into sheet properties.

3. To create **Year** and **Month** list boxes, right-click in the empty space and click on **Select** fields. Using this option you can select multiple fields. Select **Year** and **Month** from the **Available** fields and use **Add >** to add fields to **Field Displayed in List Boxes**.

4. List boxes for **Year** and **Month** appear jumbled. You can either drag them separately or, from the **Layout** menu, select **Rearrange Sheet Objects**.

5. Move the list boxes so that they are centered. To move one space at a time, select the list boxes and use the *Ctrl* + arrow keys on your keyboard.

6. Right-click on **Year** list box and go to properties. Explore different property options under different tabs.

7. Go to the **Presentation** tab and uncheck the **Single column** checkbox. Go to the **Font** tab and change the font to **Calibri** and the font size to **11**.

8. Go to the next **Layout** tab and change **Border Width** to 0 pt. Go to the **Caption** tab and uncheck the show caption checkbox. Click **Ok** to finish.

9. Drag the **Year** list box so that it appears in one row and multiple columns.

10. Follow the same steps to format the **Month** list box. Year and month list boxes should appear as follows:

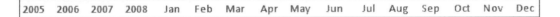

Creating list boxes for other fields

List boxes are used in filtering data. We will create list boxes so that users can use them to see specific data in the charts and tables.

Create a `Customer` list box with the following steps:

1. Right-click on the empty space on the `Dashboard` tab. Hover over **New Sheet Object** and select **List Box**.

2. A list box can be created using a field from the list or an expression. An expression is used to define the calculated field. It can involve one or more fields and can use functions.

3. From the **Field** dropdown, go all the way to the bottom and select **Expression**. List boxes can have expressions. In the expression editor, write the following expression to perform a string concatenation of a customer's first name and last name:

   `=FirstName &'-'&LastName`

4. Change the **Title** of the list box to `Customer`. From the **Font** tab, change the font type to **Calibri** and font size to **11**.

5. From **Layout**, change **Border Width** to **0** pt. On the **Layout** tab, the option **Show** is used for displaying the object **Always** or **Conditional**. Use a conditional expression to render an object on condition.

6. Use the **Caption** tab to display a caption for a list box or any other object. Captions can have a background and text colors. These colors are for the **Inactive** or **Active** state.

7. To change the background color, click on the **Color** button. Color can be fixed or calculated. The calculated option is used to display the color conditionally. Click on the **Fixed Color** button. It will display a color palette. You can either select the color from the color band or specify RGB values. Select the default background color in the **Inactive Caption**. You can copy and paste colors from the **Inactive Caption** to the **Active Caption**.

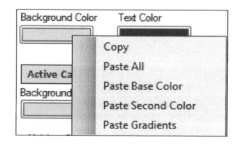

8. Caption also has options for **X-pos** and **Y-pos**, which shows where the object is placed on the sheet.

9. Use the **Width** and **Height** options to specify the width and height of the object. For the list boxes, we will choose a width of 200 and height of 100. The **Special Icons** options are used to display icons on top of the object to perform certain operations, such as send to Excel, print, and so on. Help text is used to display a help bubble for the object.

10. Sorting of the sheet object can be changed from the **Sort** tab. The following options of **Sort** exist:

    ° **State**: Sorts values according to different states of the field, for example, selected, optional, or excluded. The **Auto Ascending** option sorts and displays all values at the top of the list box, only if the list box is small and displays few values at a time and the user has to use a scroll bar to see the rest of the values. If the list box is large enough to show all the values, no sorting is applied.

    ° **Expression**: Expression can also be used to sort values as long as it results in a numeric value.

    ° **Frequency**: Sorts field values based on the number of occurrences in the dataset.

    ° **Load Order**: Sorts the fields based on the order in which they were loaded into the QlikView.

11. To make sure all the objects in the application follow the same **Caption** and **Border** properties as this list box, go to **Properties** and navigate to the **Layout** tab and click on the **Apply To** button on the upper-right corner and make the following selections:

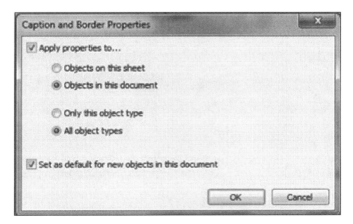

Theme can be used to create dashboards with the same look and feel. To create **Theme**, go to the **Settings** menu, and go to document properties. Create **Theme** under the **Layout** property by clicking on the **Theme Maker** button.

12. Create a new list box by selecting **ProductName** from the field list. Change the title to `Product`.

13. Create a list box by selecting **ProductLine Desc**. Change the title to **Product Line**.

14. Create a list box by selecting **Sales Person**. Change the title to `Sales Person`. Navigate to the **Expression** tab and click on **Add** on the bottom-left corner. Add the following expression:

```
num(sum(LineSalesAmount), '$#,##0.0')
```

15. This will give the sales done by each sales person. The `num` function is used to format the number.

16. Set **Width** and **Height** of the list boxes as **200** and **100** respectively.

17. Right-click on the empty space on the sheet. Choose **New Sheet Object** and select **Current Selections Box**. Set **Width** and **Height** as **200** and **100** respectively.

18. Position all the list boxes so that they line up one after the other under the current selection box on the left side of the sheet.

19. Finally, drop a **Search** object to the right. It will help in searching for any data element in the dashboard.

Options to copy and paste objects

Objects can be copied to the clipboard and pasted in the desired location. Right-click on the object and copy it to the clipboard as an **Object**.

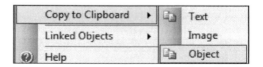

To paste the object, right-click on a desired position. There are two options for pasting. **Paste Sheet Object** means that the copied object will be pasted as a copy of the object and will be an independent object. Go to **Properties** and, in the **General** tab, see the **Object ID**. The **Object ID** of a pasted object will be different from the original one. Changes made to one object will not have any affect on the other.

Another option is **Paste Sheet Object as Link**, which creates an instance or link to the source object. When this option is used, notice the **Object ID** is the same as that of the source object. Any changes made to one object will affect the other object.

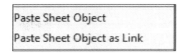

If you try to remove the linked object, you will get a warning, as follows:

Link objects are very helpful when copying and pasting a large number of objects. They are helpful in maintaining the consistency of the design.

Practice both the options by copying and pasting any object.

Placing a logo on the dashboard sheet

A logo can be added to the dashboard sheet to display the company information. A logo should be displayed based on a discussion with the users. It should be displayed based on the corporate policy of the organization:

1. Navigate to the About sheet by clicking on the **Tabrow About**. Right-click on the textbox with the image of the logo **AWC Inc**. Select **Copy to Clipboard** as object.

2. Navigate to the Dashboard sheet, right-click on the empty space and select **Paste Sheet Object as Link**.

3. Move the logo to the left-hand corner above **Current Selections**.

4. Your changes so far should appear as follows:

Creating a bar chart

A bar chart is used to compare measures. The objective of this chart is to compare Sales and Freight by ProductLine. This visualization will help them make decisions on freight. If they are spending more on freight for a specific ProductLine, they can focus on reducing it. To create a bar chart, follow these steps:

1. Right-click anywhere on the empty space on the sheet. Hover over **New Sheet Object** and select **Chart**.

2. On the **General** tab, **Bar Chart** is highlighted by default. At the top, check **Show Title in Chart** and type Sales vs Freight in the edit box. Click on **Next**.

3. On the next screen, select **ProductLineDesc** from the **Available Fields/Groups** list. Use the **Add >** button in the center to add **ProductLineDesc** to the **Used Dimensions** list. On the bottom right, uncheck **Label**. Unchecking **Label** will make sure that field name text does not appear in the x-axis of the chart.

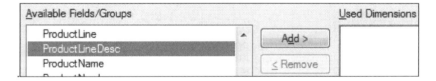

4. Click on **Next**. Explore the **Edit Expression** window. Expression should always use an aggregation function.

   The bottom half of the screen shows aggregation functions, table, and fields to be selected. The **Function** tab gives access to all the available functions. The **Variables** tab shows all the variables defined in the **Variable Overview**. **Images** shows the images available for use. These images can be used in the expression.

5. In the **Edit Expression** window, enter the expression as:

```
Sum(LineSalesAmount)
```

6. Click on **OK**. Give a label to this expression as **Sales**. Expressions can be displayed conditionally by specifying a condition in the **Conditional** edit box. At the bottom of the screen, check **Values on Data Points**.

7. Add another expression for freight and label it **Freight**:

   ```
   Sum(Freight)
   ```

8. Click on **Next**. Specify sorting on this tab. Check **Y-Value Descending**.

9. Click on **Next**. The **Style** screen shows the look and orientation of the chart. As a best practice, don't select 3D view or a glossy plot color style. Set **Horizontal** orientation and **Subtype** as grouped.

10. Click on **Next**. Review the **Presentation** properties. No changes required.

11. Click on **Next**. In the **Axes** properties, set the **Width** of the axis as **1 pt** at the top and bottom. These are for x-axis and y-axis lines.

12. Click on **Next**. On the **Colors** properties, copy the gray color from the palette and paste it on the first color on the left. The checkboxes on the right are used for different color options. **Multicolored** is used if you want different colors for the bar. **Persistent color** locks the color map so that each value has a color permanently assigned to it.

13. Click on **Next**. Provide a **Number** format to the expressions. Select **Fixed to** and specify two decimal places. Prefix the format pattern with $. At the bottom of the screen, in the **Thousand Symbol**, specify the **$K Million Symbol**, specify $M and, in the **Billion Symbol**, specific $B.

14. The font is already set to Calibri 11. Click on **Next**. No changes are required in the **Layout** properties.

15. On the **Caption** tab, uncheck **Show Caption**.

16. Click on **Finish**. Finally, move the legends on the right-most corner to any other place on the chart by selecting the chart and pressing *Ctrl + Shift*. All highlighted components can be moved. Move the legends to the top of the chart.

17. Your bar chart will look like the following chart:

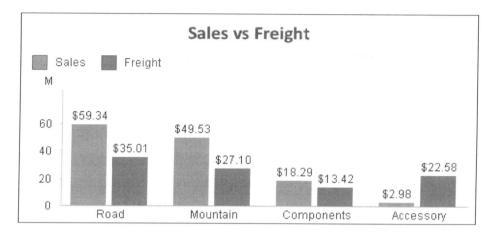

 Use **Fast Type Change** under the **General** tab to display an icon at the top of the graph to display different chart types. Users can change chart type by clicking on this icon. This icon is displayed only when the **Show Caption** checkbox is checked under the **Caption** tab.

Expression Overview

As stated earlier, **Expression Overview** manages all the expressions centrally. Invoke the expression editor by pressing *Ctrl + Alt + E* or by going into the **Settings** menu. All the expressions created so far are stored in **Expression Overview**.

Creating a text object

Text objects are a good way of displaying labels and expressions. Text objects can be made interactive by specifying **Actions** in the properties. Since we are working on a Dashboard sheet, we will create text objects to display summarized information. We will create text objects for number of Orders, number of Customers, and Total Sales:

1. Use QlikViewEssentials_Presentation.qvw.

2. Right-click on the empty space on the Dashboard sheet. Select **New Sheet Object** and then the text object.

3. On the **General** tab, in the **Text** edit box, type the following expression for # of Orders. Remember to put = in front of the expression. If you are displaying labels then you don't need =:

```
='# Orders ' & chr(10) & Num(count(distinct
OrderID),'#,##0')
Distinct is used to avoid duplicate OrderID's in the count
```

Notice chr(10) will give a line break and a calculation will appear after # Orders label. You have to format the number in the textbox using the Num function.

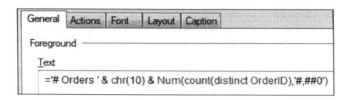

4. On the **General** tab, under **Layout** properties, set the horizontal and vertical alignment as **Center**. Set **Transparency** at the bottom left to **100%**.

5. Textboxes can have **Actions** but, for now, skip this text. Under **Font**, set the font size to **16**.

6. Create other textboxes for # of Customers and Total Sales by copying and pasting this text object and changing the calculation. You can also create a new text object.

7. For # of Customers, use the following calculation:

```
='# Customers ' & chr(10) & Num(count(distinct
CustomerID),'#,##0')
```

8. For Total Sales, use the following calculation:

```
='Total Sales ' & chr(10) &
num(Sum(LineSalesAmount)/1000000000, '$#,##0.00B')
```

To copy and paste any object, click on the object, press *Ctrl* and drag the object.

The previous text will appear like the following screenshot:

# Orders	# Customers	Total Sales
31,465	27,825	$130,146,009.19

Creating a scatter chart

Scatter charts are a good way to show relationships between measures.

When creating a scatter chart you need to specify measures for the x-axis and y-axis, and a third measure Z to display the bubble size. In this chart, we will visualize the relationship between Freight and Sales for ProductLines:

1. Use `QlikViewEssentials_Presentation.qvw`.

2. Right-click on the empty space on the `Dashboard` sheet. Select **New Sheet Object** and then **Chart**. Select the **Scatter Chart**, which is the first chart in the second row of chart types.

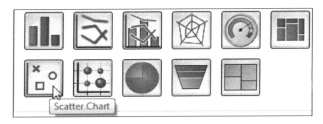

3. On the **General** tab, unselect **Show Title in Chart**.

4. Click on **Next**. Select **ProductLineDesc** as **Dimensions**. Click on **Next**.

5. In the next window for expressions, specify x-axis, y-axis, and bubble size.

6. Under **X**, pick **Freight** from the drop-down list. Specify **Label** as **Freight** %.

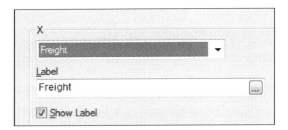

7. Under **Y**, pick **LineSalesAmount** from the drop-down list. Specify **Label** as **Sales**.

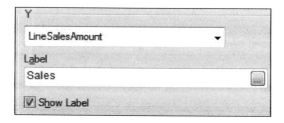

8. Under **Z**, check the bubble chart and in the bubble size expression specify `Sum(Quantity)`.

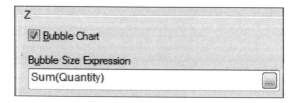

The complete expressions window should appear like the following:

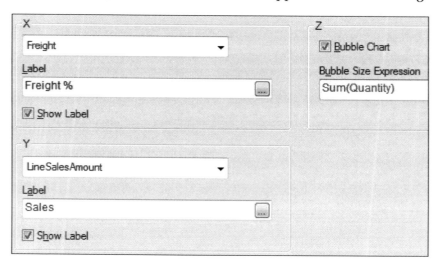

9. Check **Advanced Mode** at the bottom of this dialog box. It will display an expression in the normal expression window.

10. In the **Freight** %, expression should appear as:

    ```
    Sum(Freight)/ Sum(LineSalesAmount)
    ```

11. Check the **Relative** checkbox. This will display **Freight** % in the percent format.

12. The **Sales** expression should be Sum(LineSalesAmount) and **Quantity** should be Sum(Quantity).

13. Click on **Next** and select the default for **Sort**. Click on **Next**.

14. In the **Style** pane, pick the one with the regular bubble and click on **Next**.

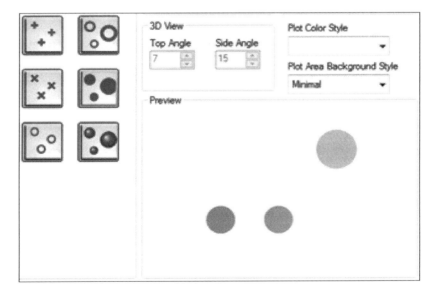

15. Select the default settings in presentation. On the **Axes** tab, on the x-axis, check **Show Grid**, and on **Axis color**, increase the width to 1 point. Make similar changes for the y-axis. At the bottom, from the **Grid Style** dropdown, pick **Thin Dashed Line**. Click on **Next**.

16. Select the default **Colors** and click on **Next**.

17. In the **Number** tab, provide the following number formatting:

    ○ For **Freight %**, select the **Integer** radio button and check **Show in percent(%)**.

    ○ For **Sales**, select **Fixed to** and specify two decimals. Under symbols, specify **K** for thousand.

    ○ For **Quantity**, select **Integer**.

18. Select default fonts and layout properties. Click on **Next** to go to **Caption**. Uncheck **Show Caption**.

19. Your scatter chart will appear as follows. Hovering over the bubble will give you the **Freight %** of **Sales** and **Sales** for a specific ProductLine.

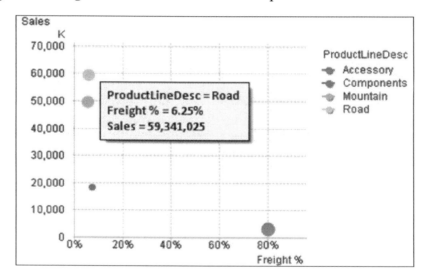

The story of two tables

In QlikView, tables are also a part of charts. There are two types of tables, straight table and pivot table.

Straight and pivot tables are used to display data in tabular format. In a pivot table, data is grouped by dimensions. Pivot tables show partial sums or sub-totals. Straight tables cannot show sub-totals. Straight tables have the dimension limits property. Pivot tables do not have dimension limits. Straight tables have the option for interactive sort.

Creating a straight table

To create a straight table, perform the following steps:

1. Right-click on any empty space on the sheet and choose **New Sheet Object** and select **Chart**. You can either create a straight table on the same `Dashboard` sheet or create a new sheet by navigating to the **Layout** menu and select **Add Sheet**.

2. On the **General** tab, specify the **Windows Title** as `Orders by ProductLine`. From the **Chart Type**, select **Straight Table** on the bottom right. Click on **Next**.

3. Set **ProductLineDesc** as **Dimension** and click on **Next** to create an expression. Label this expression as `Total Orders`.

   `Count(Distinct OrderID)`

4. Click on **Add** on the expressions window to add a new expression. Here we will create an expression to get the `# of Orders placed Online`. This expression uses Set Analysis syntax:

   `Count({$<OnlineOrderFlag = {'-1'}>}OnlineOrderFlag)`

5. Add another expression to get the `# of Orders placed by Sales Person`. This expression also uses Set Analysis syntax:

   `Count({$<OnlineOrderFlag = {0}>}OnlineOrderFlag)`

 Set Analysis is explained in detail in the next chapter. Set Analysis is used to create a "set of data". In the absence of Set Analysis, you have to create complex if-then-else statements. In the previous syntax, $ represents the current selection. Within a user's selection, it is counting the `OnlineOrderFlag` where `OnlineOrderFlag` = -1 and 0 respectively.

6. Change the text color conditionally by specifying an expression in the text color. Collapse the expression `Order` placed by `SalesPerson`. Click on the text color and write the following expression:

   ```
   if([Online Orders] > [Order placed by SalesPerson] ,red(),Green())
   ```

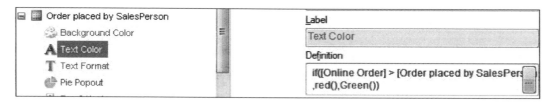

7. Select default for **Sort**.

8. In **Presentation**, make sure **Totals on First Row** is selected. Check on **Use label** and put Totals on **Multiline Settings**, check **Wrap Header Text** and specify **Header Text** as two lines. This will make sure that headers come in two lines.

9. Check defaults on other tabs and go to `Number`. For `%` of `Online Orders`, specify **Fixed** to **2** decimals.

10. Select defaults for next and go to **Caption**. Check **Show Caption**.

Enhancing your tables

Straight table expressions can have image, link, and different kinds of charts.

In the previous table:

1. Add a new expression. Label it as `Online vs Total Orders`. In the expression definition, specify:

   ```
   Column(2)/Count(OrderID)
   ```

   `Column(2)` in this table is `Online Orders`. Column numbers and labels can also be used in the expression.

2. From the representation, select **Traffic Light Gauge** and click on **Gauge Settings**.

3. Specify the **Gauge Properties**.

4. At the bottom left, uncheck **AutowidthSegments**.

5. Under **Gauge Settings**, specify the **Min** and **Max** fields. These can also have expressions.

```
Min =0
Max = Count({<OnlineOrderFlag = {'0'}>}OnlineOrderFlag)
Segment 1 Lower Bound = 0.0, Color Green
```

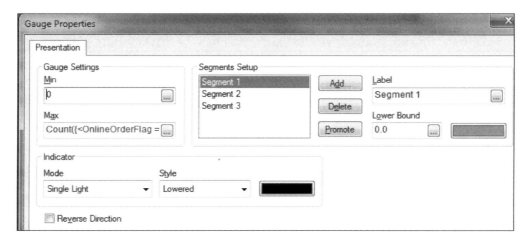

6. Similarly, specify the settings for other segments:

```
Segment 2 Lower Bound = .4, Color Yellow
Segment 3 Lower Bound = .75,Color Red
Mode is Single light, Style Lowered
```

Your straight table will appear like the following:

Orders by ProductLine					
ProductLineDesc	Total Orders	Online Orders	Order placed by SalesPerson	% of Online Orders	Online vs Total Orders
	31465	60398	76978	56.03%	◯
Accessory	19163	23358	18052	43.59%	◯
Components	4329	4590	10130	68.82%	◉
Mountain	12766	16898	22069	56.64%	◯
Road	13523	15552	26727	63.22%	◉

Groups

In QlikView, you can group dimensions and expressions. There are two kinds of group: **Drill-Down** and **Cyclic**:

- A **Drill-Down** group is created when several fields form a natural hierarchy, for example, year, month, and quarter.

- **Cyclic** groups are created to group fields that do not form a natural hierarchy. This will enable users to make quick changes to the displayed data.

Creating a drill-down group

We will create a **drill-down** group for time. This group will help users drill-down from year to month and quarter, and to perform detailed analysis:

1. To create groups, go to **Settings/Document** properties. In the **Document Properties**, go to the **Groups** tab.

2. Click on **New**. Set the **Group Name** as Time Drill. The **Drill-Down** group radio button is checked by default. Select **Year, Month**, and **Quarter** from the available fields and add to the used fields. The Time Drill drill-down group has been created.

3. You can either make a copy of the previously created straight table or work on the same table.

4. Right-click and go to properties. By clicking on **Edit Groups** at the bottom left, the Time Drill group is displayed in the **Available Fields/Groups**. Add it to the used **Dimensions**.

 Groups can be created within the chart also. On the **Dimension** tab, on the bottom left, click on **Edit Groups** and select **New**.

5. Click on **Apply** and **Ok**. Notice that the **Year** column is being added as the first column of the table. Also see a drill icon at the top of **Year**.

6. Now click on any **Year** column to drill down all the way to **Quarter**. You can also drill up.

Creating a cyclic group

Here we will create a **Cyclic** group. It will enhance the user experience by changing the dimensions between **City**, **ProductName**, and **Order Territory** with a single click:

1. To create a **Cyclic** group, go to **Settings/Document** properties. In the **Document** properties, go to the **Groups** tab.

2. Click on **New**. Set **Group Name** as Dimension Group. Make sure to check the radio button of **Cyclic** group on the right.

3. From **Available Fields**, select **City**, **ProductName**, and **Order Territory**, and add them as **Used Fields**. Click on **Ok** to close the dialog box.

4. On the previously created straight table, **Dimension Group** is available in the field list. Add this to **Used Dimensions**. Move it up next to the time period drill by using the **Promote** button in the center.

5. Notice the second column in the table as the **Cyclic** group. Click on it to change the dimensions and change the data in the table.

Creating a pivot table

Pivot tables show dimensions and expressions in rows and columns. The data in pivot tables may be grouped. Pivot tables can have partial sums:

1. Copy and paste the straight table you created previously. Right-click and go to **Properties**.

2. Under the **General** tab, change the **Windows Title** to Orders By SubCategory.

3. From the chart types, click on **Pivot Table**. This will change the table from **Straight** to **Pivot**. You can change any chart type in this way.

4. Under **Dimensions**, remove the previous dimensions and add **SubCategroyDesc** and **ProductName** as dimensions. Check **Suppress When Values is Null**. Change the labels of these dimensions to **SubCategory** and **Product** respectively.

Check that **Suppress When Values is Null** is checked so that the dimensions value will not be displayed if it contains null values.

5. In the **Expressions** pane, remove the `Online vs Total Orders` gauge chart expression.

6. Under **Presentation**, click on **SubCategory** and check the **Show Partial Sums** checkbox. Do the same for **Products**. Leave the rest as defaults.

7. Click on **Finish** and check your newly created pivot table.

8. You will see **+** in front of the **SubCategory** columns. Click on it to see the **Product** column. The table is grouped by these dimensions.

9. In the **Presentation** tab, you can check **Always fully expanded** to keep **SubCategory** and **Product** always displayed.

Container

With a little formatting, your dashboard will look like the following:

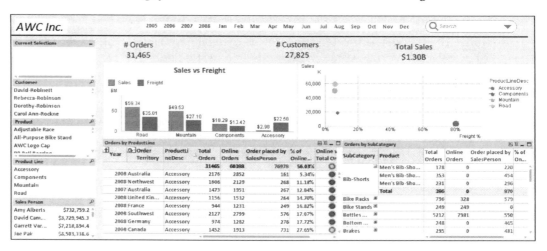

This looks a little cluttered. This can be cleaned up by using the **Container** object. Container can contain all the other sheet objects. The objects are grouped together. In the following exercise, we will put a previously created straight table and pivot table in the container:

1. On any empty space on the sheet, create a **Container** object.

2. Go to **Properties**. On the **General** tab from the list of existing objects, select the straight table `Orders By ProductLine`, and the pivot table `Orders by SubCategory`. The names of the tables will be prefixed with the object ID. Make sure to pick the right tables.

3. On the **Presentation** tab, set **Single Container Type** as **Single Object** and **Appearance** as **Tabs** at the top.

4. Click on **Ok**.

5. Once the charts are added to the container, you can remove these charts from outside.

   The **Dashboard** page will now appear as follows:

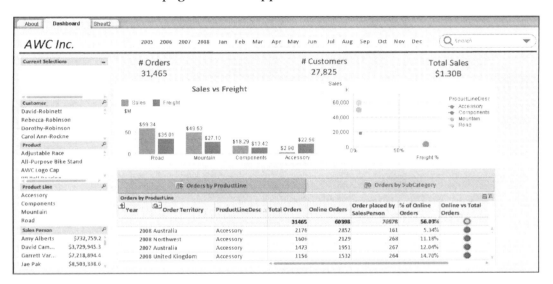

Dimension limits

Dimension limits can be set for chart types, except for gauge charts and pivot tables. It controls the number of dimension values you can see in a given chart.

Using dimension limits, you can see the first, largest, and smallest dimensions:

1. Create a new sheet. On the `Dashboard` sheet, right-click and select **Copy Sheet**. This will create a copy of the sheet. The look and feel of all the objects will be the same. You can change the title of the sheet and delete the objects you don't need.

2. You can also create a new sheet from the **Layout** menu.

3. Copy the sheet and change the title of the sheet to `Top Sales`. Right-click and remove all the charts and containers as you don't need them in this sheet. Keep the list boxes on the left.

4. We will create a bar chart to get the top five sales by subcategory. Create a new bar chart. On the **General** tab, change the title to `Top 5 Sales by SubCategory`.

5. Under **Dimensions**, select `SubCategory Desc`.

6. Under **Expressions**, specify the following expression and label it **Sales**:

   `Sum(LineSalesAmount)`

7. At the bottom, check **Values** on **Data Points**.

8. Sort by **Y-Value** descending.

9. Under **Style**, pick **Horizontal**.

10. Under **Axes**, set the **Axis** width as **1 pt**.

11. Under **Number**, set **Fixed** to 2 decimals and provide symbols **K**, **M**, and **B**.

12. Under **Caption**, uncheck **Show Caption**. Click on **Finish**.

13. Since there are so many subcategories, this chart is not clear. We will limit this chart to show just the top five subcategories.

14. Go to the **Dimension Limits** tab in **Properties**. Under **Limits**, check **Restrict which values are displayed using the first expression**.

15. Under **Show Only**, select the largest with a value of 5.

16. Under **Options**, uncheck **Show Others**.

    Your chart will appear as follows:

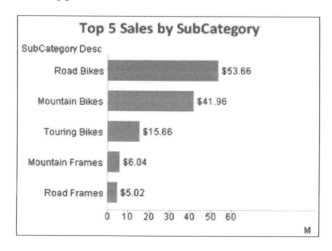

Similarly create charts for the **Top 5 SalesPerson**, **Top 5 Sales by Order Territory**, and **Top 5 Sales by Cities**. The resulting charts should look like the following:

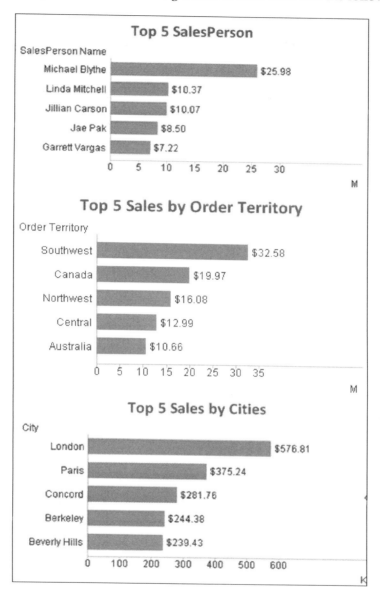

Interactivity using text objects

As mentioned in earlier sessions, Text objects can provide interactivity by using **Actions**:

1. Navigate to the **Dashboard** sheet. Go to the properties of the first text object, for example, for `# of Orders`.

2. Go to the **Actions** tab and click on **Add**. Under **Action Type**, highlight **Layout**. On the **Action** tab, select **Activate Sheet** and click **Ok**.

3. On the next screen, specify the sheet ID of the sheet that you want to activate. Provide the sheet ID of the `Top Sales` sheet. The sheet ID is `SH03`.

 Get the sheet ID by going into **Objects Properties**, under the **General** tab.

4. Now if the user clicks on the text object of `# Orders`, he will go directly to the `Top Sales` sheet where he can see the details of the `Orders`.

   Your `Top Sales` sheet will appear like the one shown in the following screenshot:

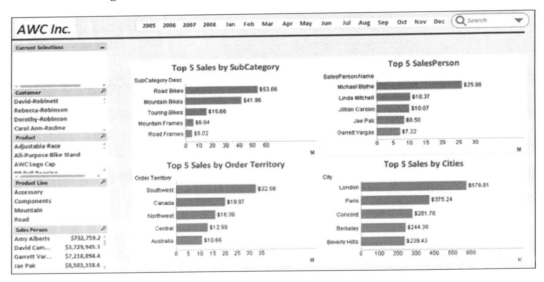

Some more charts

QlikView provides charts for all types of requirements. Here we will explore a few more charts.

Line charts

Line charts are used to display expressions in the form of lines.

1. Copy the `Top Sales` sheet and name it `More charts`. Remove the existing charts.

2. Create a new chart. Name it `Yearly Trend`. Select **Line Chart** from the chart types. A line chart is used to show the yearly trend of a measure.

3. Set **Year** as **Dimension** and expression as `Sum(LineSalesAmount)`. On the **Expression** tab, from the **Display Options**, check **Symbol** and select **Dots**.

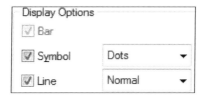

4. Under the **Presentation** tab, increase the symbol size to **4 pt**. This will make the size of the dots bigger.

5. Specify the number format as **Fixed** to 2 decimals. Specify symbols as **K**, **M** and **B**. Uncheck the **Show Caption**.

Combo charts

A combo chart is a combination of a bar and line chart. It can display one expression as a bar and another expression as a line:

1. Create a copy of the previously created line chart. Name it `Sales vs Freight`.

2. Select **Combo Chart** from the chart types. Set the **Year** as **Dimension**. Go to the **Expression** tab. You already have an expression for `Sum(LineSalesAmount)`. Create a new expression, `Sum(Freight)`. From the **Display Options**, check **Symbol** and **Line**. Previous expressions of sales will display as a bar.

3. Specify the **Number** format. The combo chart will display as follows:

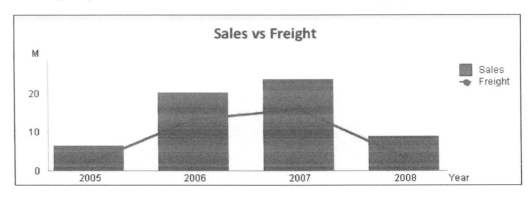

Pie charts

A pie chart is best suited when you have to display the total share by certain categories. It is best suited for a small number of categories. For meaningful results, the expression in the pie should be displayed in percentages. A pie chart will display at a glance the percentage of Sales by ProductLine. It will be better suited for higher management as they will interested in a high-level picture of the sales:

1. Create a new chart and select Pie from the chart types.

2. Select **Product Line Desc** as **Dimension**.

3. In the **Expression** field, use Sum(LineSalesAmount). Make sure to check **Relative** as it will display the expression as a percentage.

4. Under the **Style** tab, select the second style on the left.

5. Click on **Finish** and adjust the size of the chart.

6. Your pie chart will look like the following one. It shows that the product line Road is contributing the most to the sales.

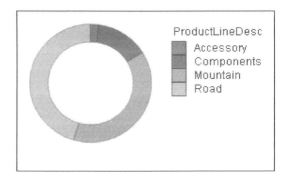

Some important functions

A variety of powerful functions are available in QlikView to be used in expressions.

The Aggr function

Aggr is a powerful function that aggregates data over the dimensions. It is similar to the Group By clause in SQL. It kind of creates a temporary table of results from which you can select and perform more aggregations. The Aggr function is used when multiple aggregation functions are required in an expression. It is similar to a chart expression based on different dimensions. Aggr can be used in expressions and dimensions:

1. Navigate to the Top Sales sheet. Go to any empty space on the sheet, right-click, and click on **Copy Sheet**. This will create a copy of the Top Sales sheet. Change the sheet name to Using Functions. Remove all the charts. Leave the list boxes of **Year, Month**, and others.

2. Create a new pivot table. Add **Year, SalesPerson Name, Product Line Desc** as **Dimensions**. Check **Suppress When Value is Null**.

3. Add Sum(LineSalesAmount) as an expression. Label it as Sales. Specify the **Number** format as **Fixed To** 2 decimals.

4. Click on **Finish** and observe your chart.

5. Now go to properties of the table. Add one more expression as follows. This uses Aggr syntax. Label this expression as Using Aggr. Leave the **Number** format fixed to 2 decimals.

   Aggr(Sum(LineSalesAmount),Year,[SalesPerson Name],ProductLineDesc)

 Notice that the result of using the Aggr and Sales calculation is the same. This is to show you how Aggr works. It is similar to chart expression over dimensions.

Nested aggregation

In QlikView, nested aggregation functions can only be used using Aggr. Now consider the requirement; there are two parts in the requirement:

- In each **Year**, find the total sale by ProductLine for each SalesPerson.

- Find the maximum sales for Year and ProductLine. In the second part of the requirement we have to ignore the SalesPerson as we only have to get the maximum sales by Year and ProductLine.

Perform the following steps to meet these requirements:

1. Use the same pivot table that we created in an earlier exercise.

2. We already have an expression in place for first part of the requirement:

    ```
    Aggr(Sum(LineSalesAmount),Year,[SalesPerson Name],
    ProductLineDesc)
    ```

3. Now to calculate maximum sales for each `Year` and `ProductLine`, we have to use the `Max` function over `Sum(LineSalesAmount)`. We know that a nested aggregation function can only be used using `Aggr`, so we will make use of the previous expression.

4. Go to the previous expression of `Aggr` and comment it. Use the following syntax, using `Max`. Your expression window should look as follows:

    ```
    Max(Aggr(Sum(LineSalesAmount)  ,Year,[SalesPerson Name],
    ProductLineDesc))

    //Aggr(Sum(LineSalesAmount),Year,[SalesPerson Name],
    ProductLineDesc)
    ```

5. You will notice that using this calculation did not change the result. This is because `Max` is calculating within the dimension of the chart, namely for `Year`, `SalesPerson Name`, and `ProductLine`, but for our requirement we need to calculate maximum sales per `Year` and `ProductLine`. We need to omit the `SalesPerson Name` dimension from the calculation.

6. Total Qualifier is used to ignore the dimension in a chart. Using Total Qualifier in the expression, you can explicitly state which dimensions to be considered in the calculation. Change the previous calculation to the following:

    ```
    Max(Total <Year, ProductLineDesc>
    Aggr(Sum(LineSalesAmount), Year,
    [SalesPerson Name],ProductLineDesc))
    ```

The total function used previously is an important function. It is used to disregard the dimension in the chart calculation. In the previous expression, the `Year` and `ProductLineDesc` fields are included in the expression, and `SalesPerson Name` is excluded because our requirement is to find maximum sales by `Year` and `ProductLine`, ignoring the `SalesPerson` in this calculation.

To further understand Total Qualifier, create a straight table and use `Year` and `ProductLine` as dimensions, and use the three expressions, shown as follows, and see the difference in the output. Use the expressions as shown in the column headers.

The first expression shows the sum by `Year` and `ProductLine`.

The second expression shows the sum by ignoring `Year` and `ProductLine`.

The third expression shows the sum by including `Year` and ignoring `ProductLine`.

Year	ProductLine	Sum (LineSalesAmount)	Sum(TOTAL (LineSalesAmount))	Sum(TOTAL<Year> (LineSalesAmount))
		130,146,009.19	130,146,009.19	130,146,009.19
2005	Accessory	58,372.49	130,146,009.19	12,555,919.99
2005	Mountain	5,944,906.61	130,146,009.19	12,555,919.99
2005	Road	6,552,640.89	130,146,009.19	12,555,919.99
2006	Accessory	604,299.30	130,146,009.19	34,940,343.11
2006	Components	92,399.67	130,146,009.19	34,940,343.11
2006	Mountain	13,967,998.45	130,146,009.19	34,940,343.11

7. To test your chart and expression, click on any **Year** and **ProductLine desc** from the list boxes.

Other functions

You can display dynamic titles in your chart using the `GetSelectedCount` and `GetFieldSelections` functions:

1. Make a copy of the previous chart.

2. Go to **Properties** and in the **Window Title** type the following command. Remember to put = in front of the statement:

```
= if (GetSelectedCount (Year) =
1, GetFieldSelections (Year), 'All')
```

3. GetSelectedCount will check whether the selection is being made in the Year list box.

4. If the selection is being made then it will display the selected field by using GetFieldSelections.

5. This will display the selections made in Year and ProductLine list boxes as the title of the chart.

6. Use GetCurrentSelections to display all the selections made by the user in any of the list boxes. Comment the previous command and type the following:

```
=GetCurrentSelections('|','=')
```

7. Sometimes, you may want to force users to select a value before rendering a chart. This can be achieved by specifying a condition in the **Calculation Condition** box in the **General** tab of the chart.

```
=GetSelectedCount(ProductLineDesc) = 1
```

8. Also click on the **Error Messages...** button and specify a **Custom Message**.

9. Select ProductLine to display the chart.

10. The chart will only be rendered if a selection is made in the ProductLine list box, otherwise it will show a message prompting users to make a selection.

Summary

In this chapter, we learned techniques for building an interactive QlikView visualization application. It started with the importance of binary load and we learned about different objects available to you for creating dashboards. We also learned about important functions required to create your application.

In the next chapter, we will learn about a very important feature of QlikView called Set Analysis. We will also learn about comparative analysis using alternate states, and techniques to accept inputs from users to perform what-if analysis.

6
Comparative Analysis

In the previous chapter we learned about creating dashboards. Dashboard applications can be made powerful by the use of comparative analysis. Comparative analysis can be best applied with the use of Set Analysis and Alternate States.

In this chapter we shall:

- Learn about comparative analysis using Set Analysis
- Learn about Alternate States
- Learn about What-If analysis using the slider and input box

Set Analysis essentials

A QlikView document is always in the current state. It shows data and aggregation on the current selections made by the user. In most dashboard applications, you have to perform aggregations or perform comparisons between the current selection/state and alternative selections or states in the chart. Set Analysis is powerful in such scenarios:

- Set Analysis is very useful for comparisons such as comparing "current year" with "previous year"
- Set Analysis can be only be used with the Aggregation function. Here we should always begin and end with curly brackets { }

Set Analysis consists of three components: Identifiers, Operators, and Modifiers:

- An Identifier defines a set. As seen in the following function declarations, `$` represents the records in the current selection and `1` represents the set of all the records in the entire document. Bookmark and Alternate States can also be used as identifiers.

  - `Sum({$}LineSalesAmount)`: This function returns sales for the current selection

  - `Sum({$1}LineSalesAmount)`: This function returns sales for the previous selection

  - `Sum({1}LineSalesAmount)`: This function returns total sales within the application, disregarding the selection but not the dimension

  - `Sum({BkMrk1}LineSalesAmount)`: This function returns sales for the bookmark `BkMrk1`

  - `Sum({State 1}LineSalesAmount)`: This function returns sales for the alternate state `1`

- Set Operators can also be used in set expressions.

  - \+ (Union): This operator returns the set of all records in the union of sets

  - \- (Exclusion): This operator returns records that belong to the first but not the other of the two sets of identifiers

  - * (Intersection): This operator returns records that belong to both of the set identifiers

  - / (Symmetric): This operator returns a set that belongs to either, but not both of the difference set identifiers

- Modifiers are used to modify a set. A modifier consists of one or several field names. They are followed by the selections that can be made in the field. Modifiers begin and end with angle brackets < >.

  ```
  Sum ({$<Year = {'2006'}>} LineSalesAmount)
  ```

  This function returns the sales for the current selection where Year = 2006.

Set Analysis expressions can use variables. In the absence of Set Analysis you have to use complex If-then statements.

Using Set Analysis

We will perform a few Set Analysis expressions to understand the power of Set Analysis. It is important for the Adventure Works company to perform a year-by-year comparison of sales. It will help them in asking questions about the years when sales went down and look for the reasons.

Use `QlikEssentials_Presentation.qvw` for this example. Navigate to the **Using Functions** tab, right click on any empty space, and select **Copy Sheet**. This will create a copy of the sheet:

1. Modify the title of the sheet as `Comparative Analysis` and remove the two tables from the sheet.

2. Create a straight table. Select **ProductLineDesc** as a dimension and label it as `Product Line`. Check Suppress When Value is Null.

3. Create an expression for sales for the year 2006. This will use the Set Analysis syntax:

    ```
    Sum({<Year = {'2006'}>}LineSalesAmount)
    ```

    Add an expression for sales for the current year and label it as `=Max(Year)`:

    ```
    Sum({<Year = {$(=Max(Year))}>}LineSalesAmount)
    ```

    Add an expression for sales for the previous year and label it as `=Max(Year) - 1`:

    ```
    Sum({<Year = {$(=Max(Year)-1)}>}LineSalesAmount)
    ```

4. Usually, selecting data elements in the list box will change the values in the table. We can ignore such selections using the following syntax:

    Add another expression, which will ignore the selections made in the Product list box:

    ```
    Sum({<Year = {'2006'}, ProductName = >}LineSalesAmount)
    ```

5. Set Analysis modifiers can also use search strings. Add another expression to calculate sales where `SubCategory Desc` like C*.

    ```
    Sum({<[SubCategory Desc] = {'C*'} >}LineSalesAmount)
    ```

6. Variables can also be used in set expressions. Go to variable overview by pressing *Ctrl + Alt + V*. Create a variable `vPrevYear`. Set the definition of the variable as:

    ```
    =Max(Year) - 1
    ```

In the straight table, add an expression and label it as `Prev Year`:

```
Sum({<Year = {$(vPrevYear)}>}LineSalesAmount)
```

7. Operators can also be used in set expressions. We will create an expression to get the sales for all the records excluding the current selection. Label this as `All - Current`.

```
Sum({ 1- $} LineSalesAmount)
```

Alternate States

Alternate States will help Adventure Works users to compare freight of different products. This was not possible until now as whenever you'd select **Product** from the list box, it'd change the data in all the charts. Alternate States provides a way to do such comparisons.

In your dashboard, you can detach any chart. Right click and choose **Detach**. Once detached, the chart will not respond to the user's selections.

Alternate States is an extension of this concept where the developer can create multiple states and apply these states to specific objects. All objects in a given state will respond to user selections made in that state. Alternate States are not available in the load script. They are a feature of a user interface.

Two states are always available in the document: the default state and the inherited state. The QlikView document is always in the default state and it is represented by $. Objects can inherit states from higher-level objects. Sheet objects inherit states from the sheet, and the sheet in turn inherits from the document.

Alternate States' functionality is invoked from document settings. Once the Alternate States functionality is invoked, the developer can create any number of states from the sheet objects:

1. Copy the Comparative Analysis sheet. Change the title to `Alternate State`. Remove all the charts from this sheet. Remove all the list boxes from the left except **Product**.

2. Go to the properties of any object and notice that **Alternate State** is not present under the **General** tab.

3. Now navigate to Document Properties from the menu. Click on the **Alternate State** button and click on **Add**. Name the `New State` as `State 1`.

4. Now go to the properties of any object and notice under the **General** tab the **Alternate State** drop-down. This can be used to assign State 1 to the object or create new states.

5. Create a new Straight table. Change the title of this chart to `State 1 - Freight`. For **Dimensions**, select **Year**, and for **Expressions**, use `Sum(Freight)`.

6. From the **General** tab, use the **Alternate States** drop-down to select **State 1**. This table is now in state 1.

7. Now selections made to any object will not have any effect on the table.

8. Now, right click on the **Product** list box. From the **General** tab, change the title to `Product-State1` and use the **Alternate State** drop-down to change its state to `State 1`. Now the **Product-State1** list box and the `State 1 - Freight` table are in the same state. They will respond only to selections made in these objects. Click on product and you can see that only the values in the table `State 1 - Freight` change.

9. Go to the properties of the **Product Line** list box. On the **General** tab, change the title to `Product-State2`. From the field drop-down, select **ProductName**. This will create a list box for **Product**.

10. On the **General** tab, from the **Alternate State** drop-down, select `<new state>`. Give the new state the name `State 2`. This list box is now in state 2.

11. Make a copy of the previously created chart. From the **General** tab, change the title to `State 2 - Freight`. From the **Alternate State** drop-down, select **State 2**. Now Product-State2 and this chart are in the same state.

12. Now remove the **Month** list box from the top. Create a copy of the **Year** list box. Assign **State 1** and **State 2** Alternate States to these charts respectively.

13. Now you can perform comparative analysis using these states. Select **2006** and **2007** in both the list boxes. Select **Cable Lock** in the **Product-State1** list box and **AWC Logo Cap** in the **Product-State2** list box.

14. Now you can compare the values in both the tables. For further analysis you can select different products in one state and compare it against the other state. For example, you can keep **Cable Lock** selected and compare it to all the other products in state 2. This is possible only because making selections in state 2 is not changing the values in state 1.

15. Your sheet will appear as follows. Notice the **Current Selections** box does not show the selections. That is because the **Current Selections** box is in an inherited state and not in state 1 or state 2. If you want to see your selections then change the state of the current selections box.

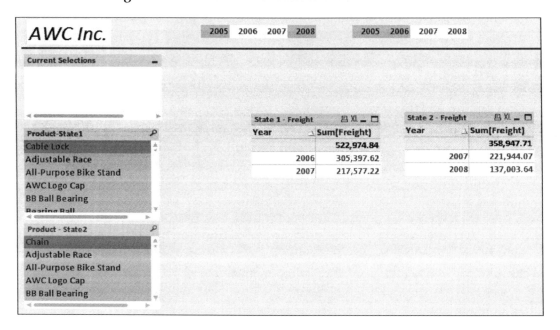

What-If Analysis

In QlikView, What-If Analysis is implemented using sliders and input box. In What-if Analysis, users can adjust the value of variables and see the effect on the data set in the chart.

Using sliders, the user wants to see how their sales amount changes if they make changes to the discount:

1. Go to the Variable Overview and create a variable vChangeAmount and set the value as .5.

2. Copy the Comparative Analysis sheet and name it What-If Analysis. Remove the table from the sheet.

3. Create a pivot table. Change the title to What-If Discount. Use ProductLineDesc and OrderID as dimensions.

4. For creating an expression, use the following and provide a Number format:

```
Sum(LineSalesAmount)        -     Label as Sales Amount
Sum(Discount)               -     Label it as Discount
Sum(LineSalesAmount) * (1 - Discount)  -     Label as
   Original Sale Amount
```

5. Create a new object by selecting **Slider/Calendar** from the list of new sheet objects.

6. On the **General** tab, the input style options are **Slider** and **Calendar**. Select **Slider**. Under **Data**, select **Variable(s)**. Select the variable as **vChangeAmount**.

7. Under **Mode**, select **Single Value**. Under **Value Mode**, select **Continuous/Numeric**.

```
Specify Min Value as .1, Max Value as 1 and Static step of .1
```

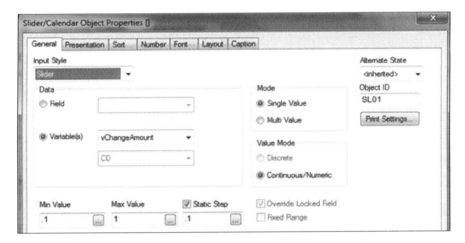

8. Now add a new expression in the table you created in step 3. Label this expression as `Target Sales Amount` and use the following code:

```
Sum(LineSalesAmount) * (1 - Discount* vChangeAmount)
```

9. Now use the slider to change the discount, which will change the value of the variable vChangeAmount and will thus change the `Target Sales Amount`.

10. For quick testing, drop a list box of **Discount** and select **$0.10**. Select **Road** from the **ProductLine** list box. Use sliders to change the value of **vChangeAmount**.

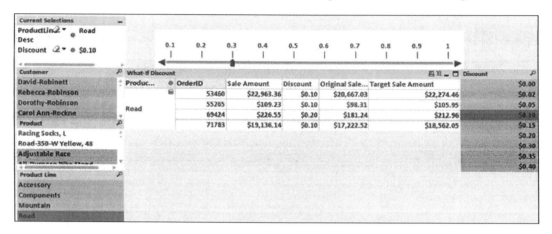

Using input box

Input box is also used to modify the value of a variable. We will use input box to change the value of freight and see how it affects the sales amount:

1. Navigate to Variable Overview by pressing *Ctrl + Alt + V* and create a variable vChangeFreight and set its value to 10.

2. Create a new object by selecting Input box from the list of new objects. On the **General** tab, change the title to Change Freight. From the available variables, select vChangeFreight and add to **Displayed Variables**.

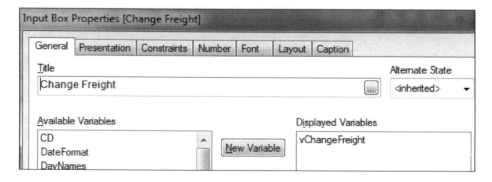

3. Create a copy of the table previously created.

4. Change the calculation of the last expression, `Target Sales Amount` to:

   `(Sum(LineSalesAmount) * (1 - Discount*vChangeAmount)) + Freight*vChangeFreight`

5. Now change the value of the freight from the input box and discount from the slider to see the changes in your target sales amount.

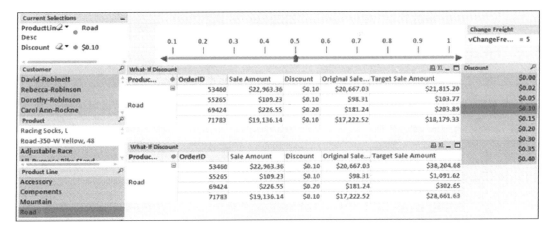

 In the previous section, two tables are created one after the other. It may happen that if you clear all the selections in your dashboard, the table at the bottom may get hidden since it will get overlaid by the chart at the top. To avoid this, either make selections in the list boxes as shown in the previous screenshot or minimize one chart, if you are not viewing it.

The last step

As the last step in your visualization application, follow these steps:

1. Navigate to the **About** sheet and create a text object.

2. On the **General** tab in the **Text edit** box, type `Get Started`. Change transparency to **100%**.

3. Under **Actions**, click **Add** and select **Action Type** as **Layout**. From the **Action** list, select **Activate Sheet**. In the **Sheet ID** box, specify the object ID of the first dashboard sheet, which is SH02.

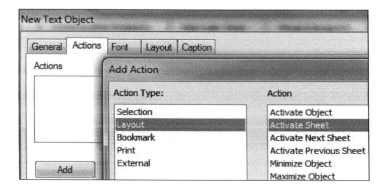

4. Under **Font**, select **Calibri Bold** and size **16**.
5. Under **Layout**, set **Shadow intensity** as **Medium**, and a **Border** width of **2 pt**.
6. Now clicking on this button will take you to the dashboard sheet.

Summary

This chapter covered Set Analysis, which is one of the most important concepts of QlikView. We also learned about Alternate States and performed What-If analysis using sliders and input boxes. We also learned about a few more chart types.

As we completed the visualization application, it is now important to secure your application.

In the next chapter, you will learn about securing your application using Section Access.

Securing Your Application

In the previous chapters you have loaded data and created a visualization application. Now it's time to secure your application so that only authorized users can view the application and data.

In this chapter, we shall:

- Learn about the overview of security in QlikView
- Learn about the different ways of securing an application
- Learn about implementing security using Section Access

In QlikView, security can be implemented in two ways. One is protecting your dashboard from unauthorized access and the other is protecting your data within your application from unauthorized access.

Application-level security is implemented at the server level where access to the dashboard application is provided based on user roles and groups. This is accomplished using the QlikView management console.

Data-level security in QlikView is implemented using Section Access. Section Access is implemented in the Qvw script. This chapter deals with implementing data-level security using Section Access.

Section Access essentials

Section Access is implemented to protect your data from unauthorized access and to ensure that users can view only authorized data.

Section Access is implemented at the document level in the Qvw script. Since the Section Access script contains information regarding user and access level, it should be written in the hidden script. The hidden script is invoked from the script editor, **File | Create Hidden Script**.

The hidden script requires a password so that it cannot be accessed by an unauthorized developer.

All access-related information can be stored and loaded from text files, database tables, or inline tables in the same way as any other data is loaded in the script.

It is important to backup your application before implementing Section Access because in case you miss the Section Access user ID and password, you cannot enter your application.

All data other than from inline tables should be loaded in upper case. Inline data is always treated as uppercase.

Section Access implements access rights based on the combination of the various criteria:

- Access: This defines the access level of the user and is a required field. There are two types of access levels, ADMIN and USER. The ADMIN controls USER privileges in the QlikView document. An ADMIN can have full authorization in the document.

- UserID: This field stores a valid user ID. QlikView will request for a user ID and compare the value in this field. User ID is not case sensitive. All fields in the Section Access definition are interpreted as uppercase.

- Password: This field contains a password. QlikView will request a password and compare with the value in this field.

- Serial This field contains a number corresponding to the QlikView serial number. QlikView will compare a user's serial number with the value in this field. This is applicable only when you are using a licensed version of QlikView. The serial can be located under the menu **Settings | User Preferences**, under the **License** tab.

- NTName: This contains a Windows NT domain username or group name. QlikView will get the log on information from the OS and compare it to the value in this field.

- NTDOMAINSID: This field contains a string corresponding to a Windows NT Domain SID.

- NTSID: This field contains a Windows NT SID.

- OMIT: This contains a field that should be omitted/removed for a specific user.

- REDUCTION: This field is used to control access to data for a specific user. The reduction field is used to compare against another field in the QlikView application with the same name. If a comparison is found, the data will be reduced for the field and will be displayed to the user.

Initial data reduction should be configured in the **Document Properties**. Using initial data reduction, QlikView removes all the data the user does not have access to, based on authorizations specified in the Section Access script. Initial data reduction is an important step in securing your document. In its absence, Section Access will be implemented without data reduction. Users having access to the document will have full access to the data.

To configure initial data reduction, navigate to **Document Properties** and then the **Opening** tab. Make sure the following settings are configured:

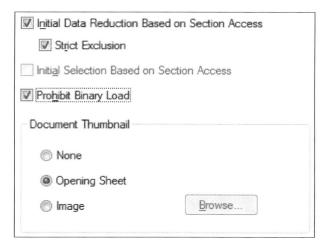

In **Document Properties**, navigate to the **Security** tab to define actions a user with user privileges can perform.

Implementing Section Access

Save `QlikViewEssentials_Presentation.qvw` as `QlikViewEssentials_Presentation_Secured.qvw`. It is important to back up your original file just in case you forget the user ID and password:

1. Open script editor and go to **File | Create Hidden Script**. Create a password for your hidden script. I used `user123`.

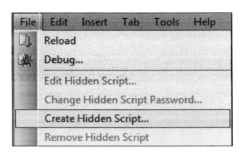

2. Type the following script and load the script:

```
Section Access;
Load * Inline [
ACCESS, USERID, PASSWORD
ADMIN, ADMIN, ADMIN
USER   U1,   U1
USER   U2,   U2
USER   U3,   U3
];
Section Application;
```

This will create a Section Access script using a `Section Access` keyword. This script is loading an `Inline` table with three columns ACCESS, USERID, and PASSWORD. You can use a database table or Excel file to load this info. This script creates four users. One user with Admin-level access and three with User-level access.

3. To test your script, close your application and open it again. It will ask for a user ID and password. Give the user ID and password as mentioned in the previous script.

4. If you log in as one of the users, go to script editor, file menu, and see that **Edit Hidden Script** is greyed out.

5. Now close your application. You may have to quit QlikView desktop and open your script again. This time log in as Admin. In the script editor, you should be able to see Edit hidden script. It will ask for a password to open the hidden script. I specified `user123` earlier as the password for the hidden script. Once the hidden script is opened we will add more options to the script.

Using OMIT

Now we will modify the script to include the `OMIT` keyword in the script. After this script, make sure to navigate to the **Document Properties | Opening** tab and check **Initial Data Reduction Based on Section Access**.

```
Section Access;
LOAD * INLINE [
    ACCESS, USERID, PASSWORD,OMIT
    ADMIN, ADMIN, ADMIN,
    USER, U1, U1, ProductName
    USER, U2, U2, Year
    USER, U3, U3, Month
    USER, U4,U4,   *
];
Section Application;
```

Using this application, user U1 will not be able to see the **Product** list box, user U2 will not be able to see the **Year** list box and user U3 will not be able to see the **Month** list box. U4 has * in the OMIT, which means that he will not be able to see **ProductName**, **Year**, and **Month** list boxes. * doesn't mean that he will NOT be able to see everything but it means that he will NOT be able to see all fields listed under OMIT:

Log in as different users and test your script. Login as user U1 and see the **Product** list box without any data.

Using reduction

Now we will use a reduction field to restrict users to seeing their own data:

Open the dashboard with an Admin user ID and password, and change the hidden script as follows. In this example, ProductLine desc is being used as the reduction field. Now user U1 will be restricted to see only data for ProductLine Road. User U2 will be restricted to seeing only the data for components.

```
Section Access;
LOAD * INLINE [
    ACCESS, USERID, PASSWORD, PRODUCTLINEDESC
    ADMIN, ADMIN, ADMIN,
    USER, U1, U1, Road
```

```
     USER, U2, U2, Components
     USER, U3, U3, Mountain
     USER, U4, U4,    *
];
Section Application;
```

Summary

In this chapter we learned about securing a QlikView application. A QlikView application can be secured at the server level and at the document level. We learned about implementing data-level security using Section Access. Now we have created a robust, secure, QlikView visualization application, it's time to deploy your application on the server so that users can view it.

In the next chapter you will learn about deploying a QlikView application on the server.

8

Application Deployment

In previous chapters, we created a data model in QlikView, we created an interactive dashboard, and applied security. Now it is time to deploy your application on the server so that users can view it through an access point/QlikView's web portal.

In this chapter we shall:

- Learn about the overview of QlikView architecture
- Learn about different components of QlikView such as server, publisher, and access point
- Have an overview of Client Access Licenses (CALs)
- Learn about how to deploy a dashboard on the server
- Learn about creating tasks, triggers, and publishing applications for the users

QlikView architecture essentials

QlikView follows a multi-tier architecture. Developers use the QlikView desktop to connect to various data sources and create data load scripts and dashboards. These qvw files are called source documents and are stored in the `Source Documents` folder on the server.

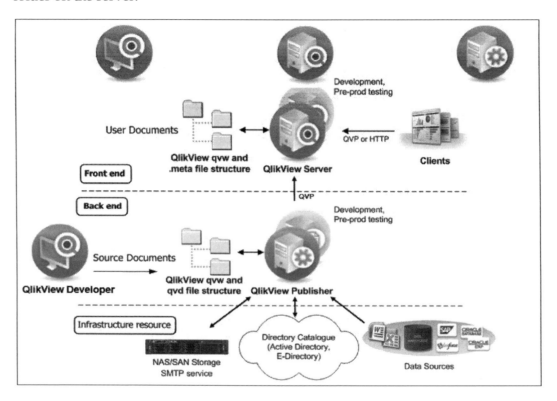

The following are the important components of the QlikView architecture:

- **QlikView Server (QVS)**: It provides a platform for hosting and sharing QlikView documents over the web portal. QVS is responsible for user management, security, and data reload functionality.

- **Publisher**: It is a component of the server and it helps in publishing the documents, securing the application, and data reduction according to the requirements. Once published, documents go into the `User Documents` folder. Users view these documents using an access point. This access point is QlikView's web portal.

- **QlikView Management Console (QMC)**: It is used to access the server and control all aspects of server deployment.

- **Access Point**: It is a web portal and is the entry point for users to view the documents hosted on the server. It presents a list of documents according to users' access rights. User access to the document is controlled by QlikView Client Access Licenses (CALs).

  Access point URLs have the following structure:

  ```
  http://<serverName>/qlikview/index.htm
  ```

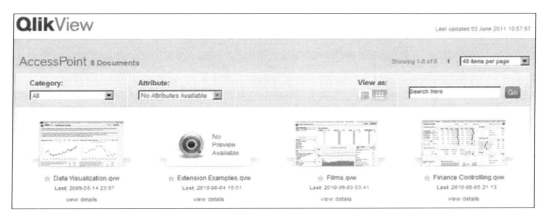

- **QlikView clients**: QlikView documents can be utilized by QlikView clients through QlikView server and the QlikView webserver. QlikView client is required for user interaction and presenting the document on the access point. QlikView has three different client types: AJAX, IE Plugin, and QlikView.exe.

Client Access Licenses (CALs)

QlikView is a licensed application, which means that to perform any operation on QlikView, users need a license. QlikView has the following types of licenses:

- **Named User CAL**: It is specific to the user or the machine. Users with this type of license can access any number of documents and for unlimited duration. This type of license is best suited for developers and designers for creating the dashboard, or dedicated users who need 24 x 7 access to the dashboard application.

- **Document CAL**: It associates users to the document instead of the QlikView server. It allows users to only access one QlikView document. This type of license is good for users who are only interested in one specific document.

- **Session CAL**: It is not tied to a specific user or a machine. Session CALs allow a single user to access multiple documents. Session CALs are used in a setup where there is a large number of non-frequent users. Users can use the license as long as it is available.

- **Usage CAL**: It gives users the ability to initiate one session, for example, accessing one document per running 28-day period. This license is also not tied to a specific user. Usage CAL and Session CAL can be used in combination.

QlikView application deployment

Once the QlikView visualization application is developed, it is deployed on the QlikView server. Users access dashboards from the server through the access point:

- QlikView applications/Qvw are developed using the QlikView Desktop. These applications contain data load scripts that generate QVDs and QlikView dashboards with visualization objects. A developer can use their desktop or laptop to develop these applications.

- Once Qvws are developed, they are placed in the Source Documents folder. A Source Documents folder is a Windows folder located on the QlikView server. A folder structure may be created and maintained to host multiple applications catering to different business units of an organization.

- The Source Documents folder and other server management operations are performed from the **QlikView Management Console (QMC)**.

- Admin or authorized developers use the QMC to create tasks. These tasks are scheduled to run data load scripts and dashboard applications.

- These dashboard applications, once run, are distributed to the User Documents folder. The User Documents folder is a Windows folder on the QlikView server. The User Documents folder is accessed from the QlikView Management Console.

- Users can access QlikView documents from the User Documents folder via the access point.

QlikView server structure

A typical server environment in QMC has different tabs:

- **System**: It gives you all the information regarding the QlikView Server and different services. **Licenses** within **System** give you information about the system licenses. Depending on the implementation, you may have just a **Server** license or a **Server and publisher** license.

- **Documents**: It provides information on the Source Documents and User Documents folder. Source Documents gives you the list of documents you have stored in the Source Documents folder. User Documents gives the list of documents published to the users.

- **Status**: It is used to check the status of the tasks executed. These tasks are for data load, that is, QVD generation and visualization generation. Using the **Status** tab you can monitor whether the tasks are successful. Status also contains a tab for services that provide information about the various services running on the server.

 Tasks are created to execute the data load and to publish the qvw. Tasks can be scheduled to run on a specific day and at a specific time.

- **Users**: It is used configure all the settings related to the users. Administrators can control Client Access Licenses, recipients, server objects, groups, and documents.

Summary

In this chapter we have learned about deploying your application on the QlikView server. We learned about different components of the server and different options available to the administrator to manage the application. This chapter also gives an understanding of different Client Access Licenses, which are important when setting up the QlikView environment. Finally, we learned about creating tasks and triggers.

With this chapter, we have reached the end of this book. In this book we have learned the full life cycle of a typical QlikView implementation.

Over the course of this book we have learned essentials pertaining to different aspects of QlikView. We have learned the complete ETL (Extract, Transform, and Load) cycle by writing scripts in script editor. We also learned how to create an interactive visualization application and learned about the use of different functions and comparative analysis. Finally, we learned about securing the application and deploying it on the server.

QlikView development is a journey and I hope by reading this book and performing all the exercises, you will be equipped to plunge into the awesomeness of QlikView.

I wish you good luck and consider you as my partner in developing applications to help the business community.

Index

database
circular reference 28
Customer table, loading 21
data, loading from 14
data, loading from Excel files 24
data, loading from text 24
data model, reviewing 38
Employee.xlsx, loading 26, 27
Exists 34
fields, creating in Order table 19, 20
If statements, using in script 35, 36
Include statement, used for including
    files 36
Inline table, loading 31
loosely coupled tables 28
OrderDetail table, loading 18, 19
OrderHeader table, loading 15-18
Productcategory table, loading 24, 25
ProductSubCategory table, loading 24
Product table, loading 21
Qualify statement 32
resident load 34
sales person, searching 34, 35
SalesTerritory table, loading 30
Shipment table, loading 30
Shippers table, loading 33
synthetic keys between Product and
    Order Detail tables, removing 23
synthetic keys, resolving 22
Table Viewer 36, 37
data model
analyzing 6
best practices 74
final model, reviewing 53
reviewing, time 38
snow flake schema 7, 8
star schema 7, 8
QlikView Data (QVD) files, adding 70, 71
development life cycle
about 5
Adventure Works Cycles 5
data model/data sources, analyzing 6
user requirements 5
development setup
about 8
Apps folder 8

Data folder 8
Images folder 8
Includes folder 8
dimension limits
about 107
interactivity, text objects used 110
using 107, 108
document CAL 138

E

EmployeeSalesTarget.xlsx
loading 57-59
Employee.xlsx
loading 26-28
Excel files
data, loading 24
Exists 34

F

fields
creating, in Order table 19, 20
files
including, with Include statement 36
path setting, with variables 64
forced concatenation option 47, 48
functions
about 113
Aggr function 113
nested aggregation functions 113-115

G

GetFieldSelections function 115, 116
GetSelectedCount function 115, 116

I

If statements
using, in script 35, 36
Include statement
used, for including files 36
Inline table
loading 31

installation
  QlikView 2-4
IntervalMatch function
  using 67-69

J

joins
  about 49
  data, aggregating 51
  inner join 49
  left join 49
  new Employees table, concatenating 51, 52
  Order 49, 50
  Order Detail 49, 50
  outer join 49
  right join 49
  working 49

K

key performance indicators (KPIs) 77

L

line charts 111
link table
  about 59
  creating 60-63
  creating, steps 59
list boxes
  creating 88-90
  logo, placing on dashboard sheet 91
  objects, copying 90, 91
  objects, pasting 90, 91
loosely coupled tables 28

M

mapping load
  CountryRegion_Inline table 45
  Product Category table 43, 44
  ProductSubcategory table 43-45
  Territory table 41-43
mapping table
  about 40

  components 40
  properties 40
master calendar 64-66
multi-tab application
  creating 84-86
  dashboard sheet 86, 87
  list boxes, creating for other fields 88-90
  logo, placing on dashboard sheet 91
  objects, copying 90, 91
  objects, pasting 90, 91

N

Named User CAL 137
no concatenate option 47, 48

O

OMIT
  used, for implementing Section Access 131
optimized load
  about 72
  conditions 73
OrderDetail table
  loading 18, 19
OrderHeader table
  loading 15-18
Order table
  fields, creating 19, 20

P

pie charts 112
pivot table
  about 101
  container 106
  creating 105
Product Category table
  about 43, 44
  loading 24-26
ProductSubcategory table
  about 43-45
  loading 24
Product table
  loading 21

V

W

Thank you for buying
QlikView Essentials

About Packt Publishing

Packt, pronounced 'packed', published its first book, *Mastering phpMyAdmin for Effective MySQL Management*, in April 2004, and subsequently continued to specialize in publishing highly focused books on specific technologies and solutions.

Our books and publications share the experiences of your fellow IT professionals in adapting and customizing today's systems, applications, and frameworks. Our solution-based books give you the knowledge and power to customize the software and technologies you're using to get the job done. Packt books are more specific and less general than the IT books you have seen in the past. Our unique business model allows us to bring you more focused information, giving you more of what you need to know, and less of what you don't.

Packt is a modern yet unique publishing company that focuses on producing quality, cutting-edge books for communities of developers, administrators, and newbies alike. For more information, please visit our website at www.packtpub.com.

About Packt Enterprise

In 2010, Packt launched two new brands, Packt Enterprise and Packt Open Source, in order to continue its focus on specialization. This book is part of the Packt Enterprise brand, home to books published on enterprise software – software created by major vendors, including (but not limited to) IBM, Microsoft, and Oracle, often for use in other corporations. Its titles will offer information relevant to a range of users of this software, including administrators, developers, architects, and end users.

Writing for Packt

We welcome all inquiries from people who are interested in authoring. Book proposals should be sent to author@packtpub.com. If your book idea is still at an early stage and you would like to discuss it first before writing a formal book proposal, then please contact us; one of our commissioning editors will get in touch with you.

We're not just looking for published authors; if you have strong technical skills but no writing experience, our experienced editors can help you develop a writing career, or simply get some additional reward for your expertise.

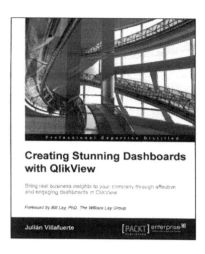

Creating Stunning Dashboards with QlikView

Creating Stunning Dashboards with QlikView

Bring real business insights to your company through effective and engaging dashboards in QlikView

Foreword by Bill Lay, PhD. The William Lay Group

Julián Villafuerte

Creating Stunning Dashboards with QlikView

ISBN: 978-1-78217-573-5   Paperback: 188 pages

Bring real business insights to your company through effective and engaging dashboards in QlikView

1. Build outstanding dashboards that respond to your company's information needs.

2. Present the data in efficient and innovative ways to promote insights.

3. Unleash the true power of QlikView by creating engaging visualizations.

Learning Qlik® Sense
The Official Guide

Get to grips with the vision of Qlik Sense for next generation business intelligence and data discovery

Qlik Q | Sense

Christopher Ilacqua   Henric Cronström
James Richardson

Learning Qlik® Sense
The Official Guide

ISBN: 978-1-78217-335-9   Paperback: 230 pages

Get to grips with the vision of Qlik Sense for next generation business intelligence and data discovery

1. Get insider insight on Qlik Sense and its new approach to business intelligence.

2. ECreate your own Qlik Sense applications, and administer server architecture.

3. Explore practical demonstrations for utilizing Qlik Sense to discover data for sales, human resources, and more.

Mastering QlikView

ISBN: 978-1-78217-329-8   Paperback: 422 pages

Unleash the power of QlikView and Qlik Sense to make optimum use of data for Business Intelligence

1. Let QlikView help you use Business Intelligence and data more effectively.

2. Learn how to use this leading BI solution to visualize, share and communicate insights.

3. Discover advanced expressions and scripting techniques that will help you get more from QlikView.

QlikView Unlocked

ISBN: 978-1-78528-512-7   Paperback: 196 pages

Unlock more than 50 amazing tips and tricks to enhance your QlikView skills

1. Learn QlikView development best practices from the experts.

2. Discover valuable tips, tricks, and undocumented features.

3. A fast-paced guide with techniques and best practices to optimize high-performance, robust, and scalable application.

Please check **www.PacktPub.com** for information on our titles

Made in the USA
Lexington, KY
28 March 2017